The Party Cookbook

Contents

Text by Peter Jeeves
Recipes by Lisa Anderson
Food Preparation by Jennie Reekie
Pictures Supplied by:
Michael Boys: 21, 28
Picture Library: 38
Christian Delu/PAF International: 40
Conway Picture Library: 58
All other photography: Bryce Attwell
Styling: Sue Laidlaw
Illustrations: Susan Richards

The Party Book was produced for Marshall Cavendish Limited by Spectator Publications Limited,

Published by Marshall Cavendish Books Limited
58 Old Compton Street, London W1V 5PA

First printing 1973 (softback)
Second printing 1976 (hardback)
Third printing 1982 (hardback)

Printed and bound by L.E.G.O., Vicenza, Italy

ISBN 0 85685 197 3

Key to Symbols

✡ This is a guide to each recipe's preparation and cooking

✡ Easy

✡ ✡ Requires special care

✡ ✡ ✡ Complicated

① This is a guide to the cost of each dish and will, of course, vary according to region and season

① Inexpensive

① ① Reasonable

① ① ① Expensive

⊠ This is a guide to the preparation and cooking time required for each dish and will vary according to the skill of the individual cook

⊠ Less than 1 hour

⊠ ⊠ Between 1 hour and 2½ hours

⊠ ⊠ ⊠ Over 2½ hours

Dry Measures

British and American	Metric
1 oz.	28·3 grams (approx. 30 grams)
3 oz.	85 grams
1 lb. (16 oz.)	454 grams (approx. 500 grams or ½ **kg.**)
35 oz. (2 lb. 3 oz.)	1000 grams or 1 kg.

Liquid Measures

British	American	Metric
⅙ fl. oz.	1 teaspoon	5 ml. approx.
½ fl. oz.	1 tablespoon	15 ml. approx.
1 fl. oz.	2 tablespoons	30 ml. approx.
8 fl. oz.	1 cup	2.27 dl.
10 fl. oz. (½ pint)	1¼ cups	2.83 dl.
16 fl. oz.	1 pint (2 cups)	4.5 dl. or 45 litre (approx. ½ litre)
20 fl. oz. (1 pint)	2½ cups	5.68 dl.
35 fl. oz. (2 lb. 3 oz.)	4⅓ cups	10 dl. or 1 litre

Important

Readers please note:
Equivalents for American ingredients are given in the text in square brackets.

SUPERCOOK PARTY BOOK

To prepare a glamorous centre-piece of frosted fruit, dip washed and dried fruit first into lightly beaten egg whites, and then into castor [fine] sugar. Allow to dry on greaseproof [waxed] paper.

The object of any party, be it for two or two hundred, is to have fun. Parties are people getting together to enjoy themselves, and it is the task of the host or hostess, within the bounds of their financial resources, to make this happen. Admittedly some people seem to have a natural flair for party giving, in the same way that good gardeners are said to have green fingers, but there is no magic formula for success. Even the most experienced host can find things going wrong—the refrigerator breaking down, or the wine merchants delivering the wrong wine. Such crises can happen to anyone, even with the most careful planning. Failure often results from being over-ambitious, and it is far better to choose something that you know from experience you can cook well, and which won't keep you awake at night worrying about the cost of the ingredients. Always bear in mind that the people you invite are there to meet each other, and that the food, wine and decoration are designed to create an atmosphere in which such meetings can flourish. As someone once said, 'a party is a gift to friends'. Planning and attention to detail are of course of the utmost importance however simple the party may seem to be. Leaving everything to the last minute causes frayed nerves—and, as often as not, second rate food because the required ingredients are not available in the shops. Apart from any other considerations, advanced planning means that the people you want to meet each other are more likely to do so if given enough warning, thereby producing the right balance of personalities and sexes. It is worth mentioning that single ladies who give parties always seem to have an excess of men, and vice versa. A fifty-fifty mixture tends to make for a better party, and diminishes the number of loners who need to be introduced.

Introductions

The question of introductions can assume a significance out of all proportion. Obviously when the guests arrive it is important that as many as possible are introduced. With a small party this is relatively simple, but with anything over thirty people, to attempt to take a new arrival all the way round will only interrupt the general flow of the party. A considerate host will keep scanning the guests for the first hour or so, to make sure that there are no lost souls drifting about with no one to talk to. Most parties have one or two such shy people. A thoughtful way of making them meet up with people inconspicuously is to ask their help with filling glasses, or taking round food, which will make them feel wanted as well as getting them circulating of their own free will. After the initial introductions, the party should swing along with its own momentum, the hosts simply making sure that everyone has what they want with the minimum of fuss and quietly checking that everything is in order. Giving a good party requires practice, and a wry ability to learn from one's own mistakes, and for that matter those of others. It is surprising what you can gain from making a mental note of small details in other people's homes. If a particular dish or wine seems to meet with everyone's approval, don't be afraid to ask for the recipe or the name of the supplier.

Atmosphere

Today we live in an age of informality. As the speed and complexity of life increases, the more we appreciate simplicity and an atmosphere in which it is possible to relax and unwind from the pressures of the day. Our Victorian ancestors sitting stiffly in their high-backed chairs could not have envisaged a party where guests lounged comfortably on cushions to eat their food, and yet the Romans found this the most satisfactory way of encouraging good conversation. Informality, however, should never become an excuse for careless presentation or lack of attention to detail. The fact that guests are eating from paper plates is no reason for a hurriedly thrown together salad, or a crumpled tablecloth.
In the following pages readers will find the basic guidelines for giving most kinds of party, together with a selection of menus and recipes both formal and informal. To the experienced party giver some of the advice may seem very basic, but it is surprising how easy it is to forget small details in the last minute rush to get everything together.
The gathering of people together to eat, drink and be merry is probably the oldest and most enjoyable of civilised pleasures, and there is nothing more satisfactory for the person who has done all the hard work than to see his or her friends happy and relaxed in each other's company. If the soufflé was a bit flat, or the Stilton not quite as creamy as the grocer had promised it would be, don't worry—the party will survive! Never be afraid to serve simple dishes—perfectly prepared steak and kidney pie, its crust crisp and shining, can hold its own with any of the great dishes of the world, and as the famous André Simon once said "If you have a perfect Comice pear, offer it in its natural state—it cannot be improved upon". The same rules apply to wine. If you can afford a château-bottled wine with a great name, all well and good, if not there are many very good wines which come from little known regions which are excellent value and modestly priced.

The guest list

As a general rule invitations for cocktail parties and large buffet or supper parties should be sent out not later than two weeks, and preferably three weeks, before the event.
If the party is to be reasonably formal, the most useful cards are those which simply say 'At Home' leaving all the other details of time, place and style of party to be filled in by hand. The guest's name goes at the top left hand corner. For informal parties this will simply give christian and surname—Jane Smith or Ann and Paul Jones, and your own name in the same fashion. For very formal occasions the invitation would read Miss Jane Smith or Mr and Mrs Paul Jones, and again your own name should be written in the same style. For small intimate parties it is quite in order to send a postcard giving details of time and place, and asking the recipient to confirm by telephone whether or not they can attend.

Numbers

The number of people you invite depends on the size of your room, the size of your pocket, and whether you like your parties hot, noisy and crowded or cool, quiet and sophisticated. Make a list of double the people you want to ask, balanced equally between men and women, then choose your final selection. It helps to list men in one column, women in the other. The advantage of sending out invitations early is that those who refuse may be replaced by others on the list up until the week before the party, using the telephone rather than a card. (Although it's a good idea to confirm in writing, too.) Make sure that when inviting people by telephone you make it clear what style the party is to be. These days most people are perfectly happy to wear what they please, but it can be

embarrassing for someone who may turn up in a dinner jacket for an evening barbecue where everyone else is in jeans, or vice versa.
Don't worry too much about mixing ages; in fact the most successful parties often have people of all age groups. Older women like to be flattered by younger men, and there are very few older men who will complain about too many pretty girls! If possible mix up some single people with the married couples, as young marrieds in particular tend to become engrossed in conversation about their children or the misdemeanours of their washing machines.

Two in a row
Don't forget that you can always have parties on two successive nights if you cannot cope with all your guests at one sitting. If you are hiring equipment the chances are you may only have to pay once, and bulk buying of wine may entitle you to a discount. In addition flowers will usually last for two days, and certain dishes may be made in bulk to cover both occasions.

Food and equipment
Decide well in advance the exact content of your proposed menu and stick to it. Your butcher and grocer may need advance warning if, for example, you intended to serve suckling pig at a barbecue, or a goose at Christmas, or require a whole Brie in perfect condition.
Make a list of all the things you will need—cutlery, china, glasses, linen, extra chairs and tables, serving dishes, or extra kitchen equipment, and then check this list against what you have available in your own home or can borrow from friends. Catering companies can usually supply everything you may need from teaspoons to butlers but if only a few additional items are needed, these usually can be borrowed from friends. Decide early what can be prepared the day before, and what has to be done on the day, and work out a systematic schedule which leaves at least three hours breathing space before the guests arrive.
Ideally this time can be spent in getting ready for the party, but the chances are that when you do a final run through, checking everything from the moment the guests arrive you will find a number of small details that require attention. It helps to have someone else checking with you as a fresh eye may detect things that have been overlooked.

Washing up
Don't forget washing up after the party is over. It is well to plan how everything is to be stacked, and valuable time can be saved by having extra washing up bowls available to soak cutlery, serving dishes etc, and some boxes or crates to take the strain from overloaded dustbins.
Finally check bathrooms, cloakrooms and lavatories to make sure that these are clean and have towels, soap, and so forth, and that the lights work. It is helpful to have a spare brush and comb, clothes brush and a box of tissues available. These are the kinds of small touches which show guests that you have bothered to take trouble on their behalf.

Coffee
Many cooks, and for that matter restaurateurs, who otherwise excel in culinary matters, fall down when it comes to a simple cup of coffee, despite the extensive range of equipment and blends available for the asking. For large parties the preparation and serving of fresh coffee does represent a problem and it is probably easier to use one of the more expensive instant varieties which simply need the addition of boiling water. For smaller numbers the glass Cona makes excellent coffee, although it does suffer from a high mortality rate at the hands of inexperienced washers-up. Probably the simplest and best method is to use one of the two piece aluminium expresso machines which come in a variety of sizes. By experimenting with different beans it is easy to achieve the exact strength and flavour required. By grinding your own beans as and when needed, it is possible always to have really fresh tasting coffee within a matter of minutes, since the beans themselves will keep for several months in an airtight jar.

Choosing your glasses
Anyone who is a regular party giver should start as early as possible building up a good collection of glasses. These don't have to be priceless antiques, but they should be fine enough to make drinking good wine an enjoyable experience, and the right size and shape for the drink in question. As a basis on which to build, start with a dozen stemmed glasses—Paris or tulip shaped for red or white wine, a dozen short wide tumblers with heavy bases for spirits, twelve sherry glasses which will also do for certain cocktails and port, and six or eight highball or long straight sided glasses for lager, beer or summery drinks (see pages 16 and 18).
The following chapters offer a range of hints and advice on giving most kinds of party, together with the appropriate recipes and menus. Whilst successful party giving demands good organisation and attention to detail, nothing contributes more to the general atmosphere than the mood of the host. If this is calm, relaxed and cheerful, the chances are that this feeling will be transmitted to the guests and the party will be a resounding success.

BASIC EQUIPMENT

Anyone who intends to entertain on a regular basis will need to acquire certain basic essentials in the way of equipment, which will help not only to prepare food, but also to serve it in an attractive and professional manner. Having the right equipment saves time and avoids the need to borrow from neighbours and friends. Most people nowadays do not have the space to house cutlery, china and glass for large numbers of guests, but a well organised host should be able to cope with eight or ten guests for dinner without hiring extra equipment from a caterer.

In the kitchen
Having the right tools can take much of the drudgery out of cooking. A set of good quality kitchen knives are as essential to the amateur cook as they are to the professional. Invest in one or two large, solid chopping boards, and, if possible, an efficient blender for liquidizing and shredding fruit and vegetables. Heavy saucepans and cast iron casseroles are expensive but well worth the investment, for if well maintained they will last indefinitely. A set of omelette pans, soufflé dishes in varying sizes, fine and coarse sieves, a food mill, mixing bowls, and a fish kettle are all part of the busy cook's armoury to be added to as the skill and range of the user grows. Whenever possible it is best to buy kitchen equipment from a specialist shop where you can see everything under one roof and draw on the advice of experts.

China and pottery
There is no doubt that a matching dinner service not only provides all the plates and serving dishes you need but brings a feeling of harmony to the table setting.
As a rough guide a well-stocked china cupboard should contain the following: soup plates or cups and saucers, dinner plates, side plates, dessert plates (which are normally the same size as those used for fish), tea pot, cups and saucers, coffee pot, cups and saucers, milk jugs, sugar bowls, sauceboats, large oval meat dishes and vegetable dishes.

Cutlery
Old silver, pewter and silver plate has a warm cared-for feel to it which sometimes makes it preferable to new modern cutlery. Requirements for day to day party giving might be approximately as follows: dinner, dessert, and bread-and-butter knives, dinner and dessert forks, soup, tea and dessert spoons, large serving spoons and forks, carving knife and fork, mustard, salt, and pepper sets, cream jug and candlesticks. Fish knives and forks are becoming less essential these days, and unless you particularly want them, use dessert knives and forks instead.

Glasses
Basically three types of glass will cover most party requirements: a Paris or tulip-shaped wine glass, a short heavy based tumbler or whisky glass, and a small stemmed glass for sherry, port and brandy. However, if you wish to add more glass to your collection, start with some extra fine tall wine glasses for special occasions, a set of stemmed hock glasses, some brandy balloons, tall highball glasses for long drinks, and finally a set of long narrow tulip shaped glasses for champagne. In addition, an ideal household will have at least two tall jugs for mixing drinks, plus a glass or silver punch bowl and ladle!

Equipment in the 'bar'
Making good mixed drinks and cocktails requires one or two items of basic equipment. A small board and sharp serated edged knife for cutting fruit, a insulated ice bucket, a metal or glass cocktail shaker, a set of bar measures or pourers, a long handled 'cocktail spoon', extra rubber or metal ice trays, a strainer to hold back fruit and ice when pouring mixed drinks from a jug, bottle and can openers and, of course, a good corkscrew.
Today's canned and bottled fruit juices are excellent, but never seem to taste quite as good as the real thing. An electrical or manual fruit juice extractor is probably the answer. Anyone giving regular parties might also consider investing in an appliance for producing home made mixers like soda water and ginger beer. These are also very useful for children's parties, when they can be made to produce cream soda and ginger beer.

The caterers
If you're going all out, a good catering firm should be able to supply anything you need for any sort of party. Large or small tents, small gold chairs, tea urns, china, linen, glass, silver, floodlighting, flowers, music and of course staff. It is advisable to contact them as early as possible especially at busy times of the year like Christmas. For large parties always ask for a written quote, which apart from anything else provides a useful check list for the host. If the company is providing food and drink ask for alternatively priced menus. Catering companies usually charge the full retail price on wines and spirits, so it is often an economy to order drink through a wine merchant who will give a quantity discount.

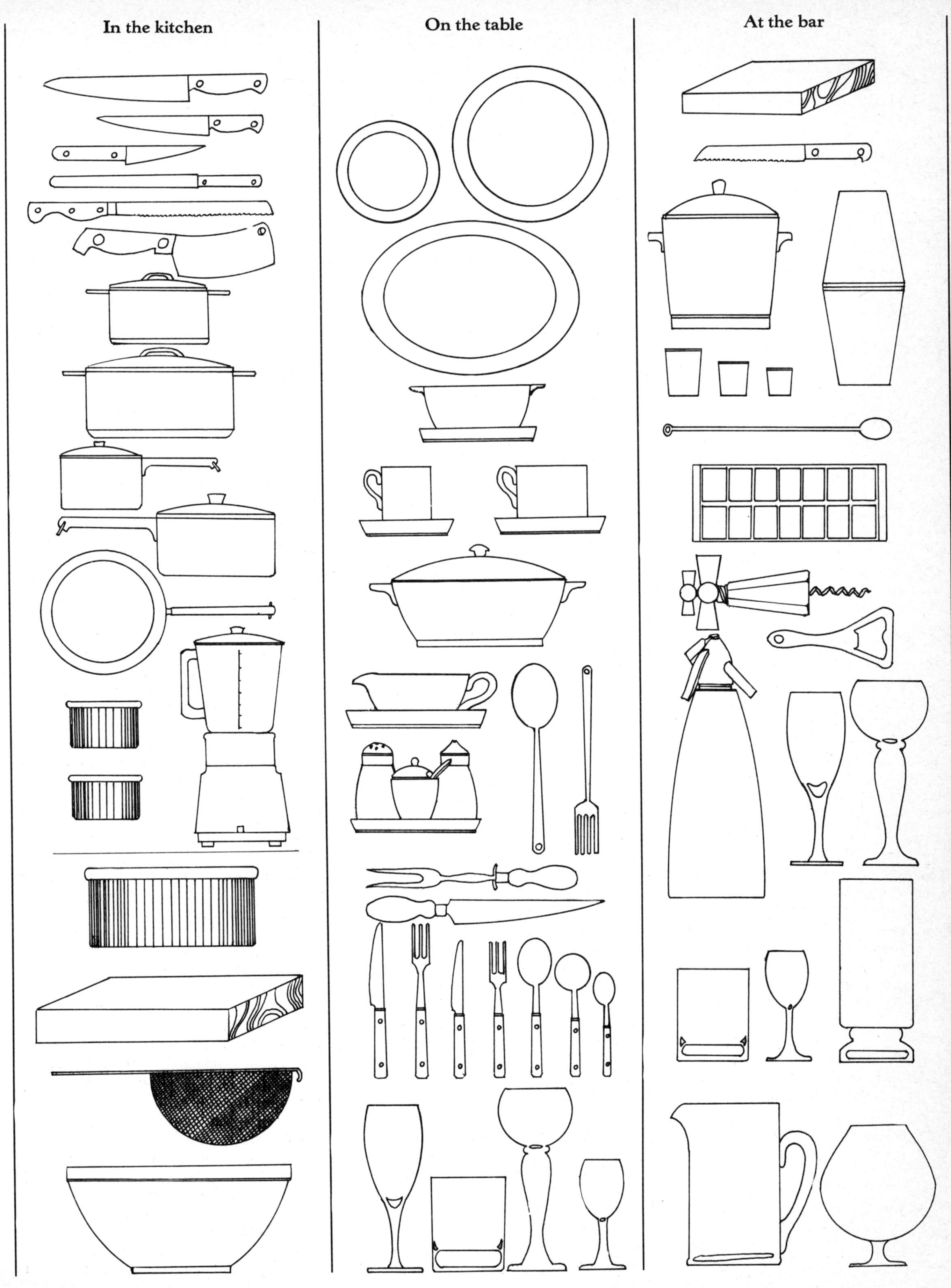
In the kitchen
On the table
At the bar

MOOD & TABLE SETTINGS

Mood settings

Creating the mood in which your party may flourish is a far more important skill than an ability to produce the perfect soufflé. Guests need the right atmosphere in order to relax and entertain each other.
The art of entertaining—and it is an art—lies in the ability of the host or hostess to mix colour, light, food and drink and perhaps music with people—in a way which produces that magic combination known as a successful party.

Colour

Colour is the basic key to all decorative themes—and how and where it is used will determine the final effect that is achieved. Bright, clear colours in china and linen can do as much for a table as any amount of flowers. Use exciting and contrasting colours like pinks, oranges and reds for informal settings; more subtle combinations for formal occasions. Try following a black and white theme on the table with all the colour concentrated in one huge bowl of daffodils or lemons in the centre. Use brightly coloured gingham tablecloths outdoors with zingy table mats and napkins in different colours for each place.
Make use of the natural colours of fruit and vegetables to add splashes of colour to kitchen, dining room or garden settings. An old flowered china bowl filled with parsley, freshly scrubbed potatoes, baby turnips and radishes will provide a perfect inexpensive centrepiece for the country lunch party or buffet table.

Lighting

One of the quickest ways of getting one's guests to relax is to create warm, subtle lighting effects that make them feel they are looking their best. The problem is to balance the strength of light, so that as well as flattering it provides a practical illumination where necessary.
Candles and oil lamps are probably the ideal way of obtaining the required effect for buffet and dinner parties both indoors and out. Fat candles last longer than thin ones, and are less inclined to tip over, especially if they are clustered together half a dozen at a time.
The old fashioned china or brass oil lamps can also be dotted around in gloomy corners, or used to light landings and staircases in winter. Make sure the wicks are well-trimmed, to achieve a really sharp light and minimize the odour of burning paraffin. If you are lucky enough to have a swimming pool, or even a small ornamental pond in the garden, try floating a dozen or so small night lights on coffee saucers over the surface. The effect can be quite magical on a warm summer evening.

Music

Background music can be very pleasant if it is really in the background, and doesn't intrude on conversation. A touch of quiet music after dinner can make a delightful interlude in an evening round the fire with coffee and liqueurs.
Cocktail parties for some inexplicable reason seem to benefit from a gentle musical accompaniment, although changing records can become tiresome extra responsibility for a busy host or hostess. Delegate this duty to a reliable friend, if you can.
For large parties or special celebrations like twenty-first birthdays you might consider it worthwhile to hire a mobile discotheque which comes complete with its own disc jockey rather than rely on your tape recorder or stereo. If your preference is for live music it is usually possible to engage the services of a local group, who will usually prove inexpensive if their fame is yet to come!

Flowers

Fresh flowers and plants are the best possible way to make a home hospitable. With their colour, warmth and perfume they welcome your guests in every room, and help to bring the dreariest corner and alcove to life.
The ability to arrange flowers is more a question of having an eye for colour and shape than a textbook knowledge of technique. In fact the simplest arrangements are usually by far the best—and infinitely more effective than the rather static affairs in which most flower shops seem to specialize. A simple bowl of field flowers, a perfect camelia in a wine glass, wild poppies or daisies in a stone jug, a bunch of violets or rosebuds in an old cut-glass scent bottle—these are the arrangements that catch the eye.
For the country dweller flower decoration is a relatively simple and inexpensive business, since apart from in the very depths of winter there are usually leaves, blossom, grasses, ferns and wild flowers available to decorate the house for a party. Even the kitchen garden will yield huge jagged-edged artichoke and rhubarb leaves, onion flowers, parsley, asparagus fern, and bushy green fennel tops.
Whatever flowers or plants you use for decoration, arrange them to create an aura of warmth, colour and dramatic effect.

Eating out of doors

Eating out of doors can be a beach party for teenagers, a barbecue in a town garden, dinner for two on a balcony or a pool party under the stars. Whatever the style the important points are to create a colourful *al fresco* atmosphere, to

right: The richly-hued tablecloth and napkin are given extra impact with a bowl of bright flowers.
below: A formal setting creates an elegant impression—here, by using heavy silver and cut glass on a mahogany table.

ensure that guests can eat and drink in comfort, and if possible to have an alternative arrangement which would cover a sudden change in the weather. Use brightly coloured tablecloths and napkins, china with fruit and vegetable designs and motifs; big cushions or air mattresses covered with rugs. Make use of pots and tubs filled with plants to provide extra colour, hang ferns from the roof of the veranda or porch. Fill the wheelbarrow with fruit, vegetables and wild flowers and make improvised floor lights by sticking light bulbs in flower pots to illuminate pretty shrubs and statues or a trellis at night. Edge steps, paths and driveways with night lights in coloured jars—or for children, scooped-out grapefruit or watermelons with cut-out faces.

Dinner for two

For two people who really enjoy each other's company a long relaxed dinner can be the perfect way to spend an evening. If you are organising dinner, make sure you choose the other's favourite things to eat and drink. In winter make sure the room is cosy and warm with soft lighting, and free of cooking smells. In summer have it fresh and cool, with lots of flowers.
A woman can show her culinary talents in small ways; perhaps a loaf of home made bread, butter sculptured with a special initial or design, or after-dinner peppermints she has made herself. Bachelors may find themselves short of menu ideas, or for that matter some of the more elegant embellishments for the table.
A good start to the evening is a bottle of champagne in the refrigerator. Whatever party you are giving be it dinner for twenty or supper for four, the atmosphere you create will come from your own personal enjoyment of entertaining your guests.

right: A bright and gay atmosphere may be created inexpensively by using colour co-ordinated disposable plates, mugs and napkins.
below: A dramatic and unusual table setting puts fresh scrubbed vegetables to good effect as a centrepiece, and echoes their colours and texture in china and table linen.

Table settings
One of the most enjoyable and satisfying aspects of entertaining lies in creating an attractive table setting for your guests. Whether the occasion is grand or informal, table settings reflect the care and attention to detail which are the hallmarks of a good host.
Changing patterns of living and entertaining, however, have generated a much more relaxed attitude towards what goes on the table, and today's table setting accessories are chosen for their versatility and practicality rather than their opulence. Luckily manufacturers and designers are well aware of the need to make life simple, and consequently have produced linen that is easy to wash and iron, china and glass that will stand up to the rigours of the washing machine, and ovenware that not only cooks well but makes its own colourful contribution to the table.

Matching china
Shops today carry a wide range of excellent and inexpensive china, from which it is possible to build up one's collection a few pieces at a time.
As a general rule dinner or luncheon plates should match side plates in order to give the table cohesion. Soup cups or bowls, dessert plates and serving dishes, however, may be of a different design, colour and texture as long as they are basically complementary to the overall setting.

How to set your table
How you set your table is determined to a large extent by the style of party and type of food you are serving. For example, a country buffet lunch of steak and kidney pie and treacle tart looks very much at home set out on an oak or scrubbed pine table, using old willow patterned plates and

right: A group of large candles will provide light where it's needed, and will lend a warm glow to the table.
below: Here a patchwork-effect cloth provides a colourful background to carefully co-ordinated accessories.

earthenware jugs for wine and cider. If the same party were held in a town house or flat, the food might be a little more sophisticated and consequently you may feel a more formal table setting is required.

Choosing a centrepiece
Every party table setting should have a centrepiece which creates a dramatic colourful effect and helps to draw everything, including the guests, together. This may be achieved with flowers or plants, or a magnificent composition of fresh fruit, a beautiful piece of china or glass, a mound of dried gourds or freshly scrubbed vegetables, a fine tureen or punchbowl. Alternatively use a special first course such as a huge pyramid of giant prawns or shrimp on crushed ice, or a mound of watermelon slices. Whatever you use make sure it allows guests on either side of the table to converse without craning their necks.

Linen
Today it is possible to select linen from an almost limitless choice of colours and designs which means that settings can be easily varied according to the mood and style of the party. Use stripes, checks, floral patterns or polka dots either on their own or covered with see-through lace. Contrast dark rich-hued cloths with mats in brightly coloured straw or papier maché, with napkins to match. Use two cloths on one table—a heavy embroidered bedspread or quilt to the floor, overlaid with old fashioned lace or damask. Or (especially for a round table) use a short cloth in matching fabric over the full-length cloth, which is itself covered with clear plastic. This cuts down dramatically on washing and ironing! For a change try keeping everything on the table the same colour as your

right: A perfect breakfast or brunch setting in a cool and crisp combination of yellow and white.
below: For a children's party, the clown theme is carried through from the sensible disposable cups, plates and napkins to a truly splendid cake.

china—say dark green tablecloth with matching napkins and place mats of a lighter shade. The overall dark background can then be used to offset a dramatic eyecatching centrepiece of white flowers.

Finishing off the table

There are one or two small touches which help give the table a finished look. Napkins can be slightly starched and look very good stuffed neatly into glasses, so that the edges overhang in folds. Or try the 'mitre' fold—fold each napkin in half to make a triangle, then bring the longest side (the folded edge) two-thirds of the way up, and crease it neatly. Turn the napkin over, hold one end between thumb and palm, and wrap it around the hand. Tuck the free end over the top of the band, and tuck it in neatly.

It is a nice touch to give each guest a small separate dish of butter, and long Italian breadsticks set at intervals look attractive and help people on diets. Make sure there are plenty of ashtrays, and if you feel generous, cigarettes.

Ideally guests should have two glasses, one for red and one for white wine—plus a sherry glass if you wish to be very formal and serve this with the first course. Port, brandy and liqueur glasses are kept to one side and produced when the table has been cleared for coffee.

Looking for antiques

Old silver, glass and china can give character to a table setting, and it is surprising how easy it is to pick up odd inexpensive pieces here and there by browsing around antique and junk shops. Pewter plates, for example, make excellent place mats, big Victorian-style flowered pitchers can be used for serving summer drinks, or the matching bowl for salads.

HINTS ON WINE

Wine drinking is, simply, a delightful and relaxing pastime which enhances the enjoyment of good food. Regretfully the subject is all too often cloaked in a totally unnecessary mystique.

The wine merchant
Seek the services of a reputable wine merchant. Like a lawyer the wine merchant's job is to advise. Discuss with him the style of party you are planning, the menu you have chosen, and above all the budget you have available. Only by knowing the facts can he select the right wine to suit your own particular needs.
Buying wine for parties falls roughly into two categories—those for informal occasions, like the small luncheon or dinner party—and wines for very special occasions.
In Europe it is possible to buy wines in the first category relatively inexpensively, the best coming from France and Germany, followed by those from Italy, Spain, Portugal and Austria. Quality will depend to a large extent on the skill and reliability of the shipper, and it may well be necessary to try several names, before finding wines that are consistently good.
In countries where imported wines are scarce and expensive, there are usually regional wines which are excellent value for every day drinking and which often compare favourably with their European counterparts.
But for special occasions it is a great compliment to your guests to offer them one of the great wines from a famous Château, a magnificent Estate bottled wine from Germany, or a vintage Champagne.

Serving wine
As a general rule, red wine should be served at room temperature (60°F); white wines and *vin rosé* slightly

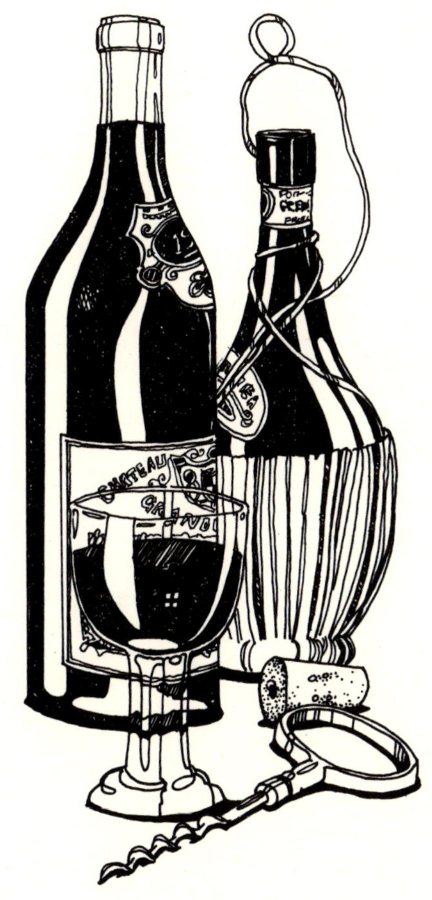

chilled (50°F), so that they taste cool but not cold in the mouth.
Red wines with any degree of age should always be decanted, a procedure which allows the wine to breathe, and at the same time removes any deposit which may have formed at the bottom of the bottle. Decanting should be done slowly, preferably using a strainer, approximately two hours before serving. Even cheap red wines benefit from having their corks removed, and being allowed to stand in a warm atmosphere prior to drinking. With older wines it is advisable to clean the inside and outside of the neck with a dry cloth before serving or decanting.

What to serve with what
Choosing the right wine to go with a particular dish is largely a question of practice and personal preference. It is best to keep château-bottled wines for rather grand occasions when you may be serving a rich or lavish main course.
Most starters and especially soups are improved by the accompaniment of a glass of Fino or Amontillado sherry, or Madeira. Shell fish like oysters or mussels, smoked trout, eel or fish pâté benefit from a good dry white wine like Chablis. Red meat and game are best matched with a big fruity red like a Burgundy or Rhône; while lamb, chicken and veal dishes, and pork, are better with a lighter Claret or a robust white wine with plenty of character. Plain simple fish dishes go best with a wine with rather a strong appeal, such as Sancerre, or a dry but soft-tasting wine such as Muscadet. Where rich creamy sauces are involved try a wine with a slight sharpness to it, like Rhine or Moselle.
Serving a sweet wine with dessert is a custom which seems to be gaining in popularity around the world. Good sweet wines are expensive but one glass with fruit or a fruit based sweet is a magical experience.

Keeping a note
Making a note of wines that you have enjoyed outside your own home is a good way of building a small personal reference library. Brief details of year, region and shipper's name can be jotted down and referred to at a later date. It is also useful to acquire a small pocket vintage chart which will tell you at a glance the quality of wine in any year.

HOME FREEZER ENTERTAINING

Anyone who owns a home freezer will be only too delighted to tell you what a difference it can make to home entertaining. They will tell you about the vast range of dishes which may be cooked and frozen weeks—or even months—in advance, and of the pleasures of eating certain fruits and vegetables out of season. But above all, they will stress the appliance's value as a time and money saver.

The advantages
Home freezing is not difficult, and—contrary to popular opinion—is not only of benefit to those of us lucky enough to own bountiful kitchen gardens. Owning a freezer means that shopping trips can be made less frequently, and savings of up to a third of normal prices may often be made, by buying commercially frozen foods in bulk. One of the great advantages of the home freezer is that it may be used to store a wide variety of cooked or prepared appetizers, main courses and desserts, suitable for all types of parties. This cuts down to a minimum the time that must be spent in cooking for a lunch, dinner or buffet party, and so allows you to devote far more attention to getting your home into good order, and to arranging flowers and table settings. A well-stocked freezer also allows you to cope quickly and efficiently with friends who drop in for a meal without warning.

Buy now—eat later
Being able to store perishable foods for long periods is especially advantageous for the party-giver—for it enables the purchase of special foods when they are fresh, at the peak of their season, and in perfect condition. Even such delicacies as asparagus, salmon or raspberries may be obtained at relatively cheap prices, and later served to delighted guests, perhaps in mid-winter. Game such as grouse, pheasant, wild duck, hare and venison may all be bought in the autumn, frozen and later produced for special occasions—either in their natural state, or made up into casseroles and pâtés. Strawberries, plums and blackcurrants may all be tucked away in the home freezer, to be brought out at a later date for fruit fools, ice-creams or sorbets. Avocados may be made into a delicious soup or dip for use weeks later; and hamburgers may be prepared in bulk, perhaps for hungry teenagers who may suddenly feel like an impromptu barbecue. Curries, flans, casseroles and pies are all standbys which can be used for dinner parties, or as a hot dish for a buffet or a late-night supper. Homemade bread and pastry may be successfully kept in the freezer for several weeks, and make a useful addition to the emergency store cupboard. And cranberry sauce, mince pies, and rum and brandy butter may all be made weeks in advance, to save time during those vital days before Christmas or Thanksgiving.
Squeezing and freezing your own fruit juice is a guaranteed way of getting the really natural flavour of fresh fruit. Orange, grapefruit, and tomato are all ideal for freezing, and are especially useful if you are intending to make mixed drinks, or for a children's party. Try freezing these pure juices into cubes too—these look and taste very good in drinks. (A cube of pineapple added to tomato juice, or to coke, for example.)
It is also an excellent idea to flavour water for ice-cubes before freezing, with a little lemon or orange juice, and to add thinly peeled zest, or a slice of the fruit itself, to each cube compartment before freezing. It looks very special indeed, and takes very little time to prepare. Use the juice from a lemon or orange to flavour about 1 pint [2½ cups] water. Garnishes such as croûtons—or any other fried bread shapes—and fresh breadcrumbs will come in very useful if packed away in the freezer. Croûtons need to be reheated in the oven at 400°F (Gas Mark 6, 200°C) for about 5 minutes, but need not be defrosted beforehand. Fresh herbs, such as parsley, may be stored in plastic bags—or pressed tightly into ice-cube trays. Most herbs don't need to be pre-chopped, because the leaves may be crumbled up if necessary while still frozen.

What can be frozen
Most foods can be successfully frozen, as long as the quality is good, and care is taken to prepare and package everything exactly according to instructions. But naturally there are some foods which do not lend themselves to freezing. Lettuces, watercress and other salad greens never regain their original crispness; single cream (or any with a butter fat content of less than 40%) will separate when defrosted. Other foods which should be avoided are custards, mayonnaise, eggs in their shells (or hard-boiled eggs), icings and frostings, and soft fruits such as bananas.
Remember too that freezing food will never improve its texture—and so, although frozen food could be kept for long periods of time, it is best eaten within the recommended periods.

HOW MUCH FOR HOW MANY

	Single serving	24 servings	Notes
Meat with bone	5-6 oz.	7-9 lb.	For buffets or barbecues—cold roasts, chops, chicken pieces
Meat without bone	4-5 oz.	6-7 lb.	For buffets or barbecues—casseroles, steaks, stews, pies
Pâté	3-4 oz.	5½-6½ lb.	For serving at wine and cheese parties, or drinks parties
Salad vegetables:			
lettuce or curly endive [chicory]	1/6 average	4-5 lettuces	Add dressing at last minute
white or red cabbage	1 oz.	1½ lb.	For a mixed salad bowl
cucumber	1 inch	2 cucumbers	
tomatoes	1-2	3 lb.	
raw cauliflower	1-2 oz.	1½-3 lb.	
Salad dressings:			
mayonnaise	1½-2 fl. oz.	1½-2 pints [3¾-5 cups]	see page 62
french dressing	1 fl. oz.	1-1½ pints [2½-3¾ cups]	To make 1 pint, [2½ cups] shake together (in a tightly lidded container) 5 fl. oz. [⅝ cup] tarragon or cider vinegar, 10 fl. oz. [1¼ cups] oil, 1 clove of garlic, finely crushed, 4 teaspoons sugar, 1 teaspoon mustard, ½ teaspoon salt, and plenty of freshly ground black pepper.
Rice or pasta	1½-2 oz. (uncooked)	2-3 lb.	Allow 2 teaspoons salt and 1 pint [2½ cups] water for each ½ lb. long-grain rice
Coffee:			
instant, hot	1/3 pint [¾ cup]	2-3 oz. coffee 6 pints [7½ pints] water 2 pints [5 cups] milk 1 lb. sugar	Make coffee in jugs as required, and serve the milk and sugar separately.
ground, hot	1/3 pint [¾ cup]	9-10 oz. coffee 6 pints [7½ pints] water 2½ pints [6¼ cups] milk 1 lb. sugar	If the coffee is made in advance, strain after infusion, and reheat without boiling. Serve the milk and sugar separately.
instant, iced	1/3 pint [¾ cup]	3 oz. coffee 2 pints [5 cups] water 6 pints [7½ pints] milk sugar to taste	Make black coffee (half sweetened, half not) and chill. Mix with chilled creamy milk; serve in glasses.
ground, iced	1/3 pint [¾ cup]	12 oz. coffee 6 pints [7½ pints] water 3 pints [5 cups] milk sugar to taste	Make black coffee (half sweetened, half not) strain and chill. Mix with chilled creamy milk; serve in glasses.
Tea:			
Indian, hot	1/3 pint [¾ cup]	2 oz. tea 8 pints [10 pints] water 1½ pints [3¾ cups] milk 1 lb. sugar	It is better to make tea in several pots rather than one very large one. Serve the milk and sugar separately.
Indian, iced	1/3 pint [¾ cup]	3 oz. tea 8 pints [10 pints] water 1 pint [2½ cups] milk 3-4 large lemons, cut into thin slices 4 tablespoons chopped fresh mint	Strain the tea as soon as it has infused sweeten half, and chill. Serve in glasses with chilled creamy milk, slices of lemon, or mint.

MIXED DRINKS & APERITIFS

Given the basic ingredients of whisky, gin, rum and vodka it is possible to produce a whole range of exciting mixed drinks, and with the variety of vermouths, bitters and mixers available there is every reason for a host to offer a number of alternatives to the ubiquitous glass of sherry. Whatever the time of year, the ingredients for mixing exotic and unusual drinks are easy to come by. It is surprising what a difference a slice of pineapple or peach can make to the taste and appearance of a vodka and tonic, or what a long twist of orange peel and plenty of ice will do for a glass of sweet vermouth.

Gin
The number of mixed drinks and cocktails which are gin-based are legion. It is probably the most versatile of all spirits. The following is a selection of long and short gin-based drinks.

Booths Party Punch (for 12 people)
6 wine glasses gin
1 wine glass Cointreau
½ wine glass brandy
juice of 3 lemons
1 heaped tablespoon castor [fine] sugar.

Mix well together in a pitcher with a large bottle of lemonade and plenty of ice. Decorate with slices of cucumber. Serve in medium-sized tumblers or wine glasses.

Gin Fizz
1 fl. oz. gin
juice of half a lemon
½ tablespoon castor [fine] sugar

Shake well with plenty of ice, strain into a wine glass and top up with soda water.

Horse's Neck
Add to a tall highball glass a long twist of lemon peel, a double measure of dry gin and top up with ginger ale. This drink may also be made with brandy, whisky or rum.

Whisky
Whisky is probably best taken on its own or with soda or water, but the following two recipes may be useful for warming up cold guests on a winter's evening.

Whisky Mac
Mix equal quantities of Scotch whisky and ginger wine. Serve in medium-sized tumblers without ice.

Hot Toddy
Mix a double measure of whisky with the juice of half a lemon, and a teaspoon of honey, in a tall glass. Top up with hot water. (Excellent for adults who join the kids around the bonfire on Guy Fawkes' night).

Vodka
Vodka basically falls into two classes—the real thing from Russia or Poland, and the locally made. The former has a more subtle flavour, is expensive and best drunk ice cold with smoked, fish titbits. The latter is best used as a basis for any number of excellent mixed drinks, the best known—and probably the best—being the Bloody Mary.

Bloody Mary
4 fl. oz. vodka
14 fl. oz. canned tomato juice
juice of half a lemon
celery salt
black pepper
1 tablespoon Worcestershire Sauce
salt

Shake vigorously together with plenty of ice, and serve in tall glasses. These quantities should be used as guidelines, and varied according to personal preference.
A 'Bull Shot' is an excellent alternative and is made in exactly the same way, except that a can of beef consommé is substituted for tomato juice. A really delicious pre-lunch drink.

Moscow Mule
Mix a double measure of vodka in a tall glass with plenty of ice. Top up with good quality ginger beer and a dash of lime juice. Decorate with a slice of lime or lemon.

Screwdriver
2 fl. oz. vodka
1 fl. oz. orange juice
½ teaspoon castor [fine] sugar

Shake together with plenty of ice, and serve in medium-sized glasses with a slice of orange.

Rum
White rum is becoming increasingly popular as a basis for mixed drinks, but is still expensive by comparison with other spirits. It may be mixed with tonic, ginger ale, and bitter lemon in the same way as gin and vodka and produces an interesting and distinctive drink especially in summer.

Cuba Libre
2 fl. oz. white rum poured over ice cubes in a tall glass. Top up with ice-cold cola and a dash of lime juice. Decorate with a long twist of lemon peel.

Rum Nogg
2 fl. oz. dark Jamaican rum
1 egg
teaspoon of sugar
12 fl. oz. [1½ cups] milk

Shake thoroughly, strain into medium-sized glasses and finish off with a little grated nutmeg.

LIGHT-DRY
RUM

THE DRINKS PARTY

below: A little extra time is worth the effort with an hors d'oeuvres plate—here piped mayonnaise, sour cream or taramasalata is combined with slices of hard-boiled egg, cucumber or radish, or with olives, grapes or Danish caviar.

1	2	3
Cheese Aigrettes	Devils on Horseback	Sausages in Chutney Sauce
Pineapple and Cream Cheese Dip	Cheese Sputniks	Cheese-Stuffed Celery
Egg and Caviare on Black Bread	Avocado and Cheese Dip	Taramasalata on fried bread shapes
Ham and Cream Cheese Rolls	Smoked Cheese Dip	Smoked Salmon and Dill Rolls
Tuna Fish Pâté on crackers	Beef and Horseradish Rolls	Green Cheese Dip

(see index for page numbers)

Any occasion for getting together over a drink with friends may be turned into a party—whether it's cocktails, a pre-lunch Bloody Mary, beer on the beach, or an after-supper affair. People are discovering the enjoyment to be had from combining various ingredients to produce a drink that is different, and that comes as a welcome change to the traditional gin and tonic or whisky and soda.

The cocktail party
Over the years the cocktail party has gained a rather bad reputation, mostly because some hosts have used it as a means of entertaining as many people as possible at once. The result has too often been overcrowded stuffy rooms, warm drinks, and a noise level that makes conversation a nightmare! So make sure that yours is the delightful event it can—and should—be.

Planning the party
When planning a drinks party never invite more people than your room will hold comfortably. Comfortably means leaving enough space for the host (or a helper) to move easily from group to group with drinks and food. If possible set up your bar in a separate room on a long table, so that the ingredients for mixing your drinks, together with glasses, ice, bottle openers and all the other paraphenalia, may be laid out neatly and checked with a quick glance before guests arrive. Use a tin bath or similarly sized container filled with water and ice to chill spirits, mixers, fruit juice, champagne and white wine.

How much to order?
Deciding how much drink to order can be tricky. The best solution is to ask your wine merchant to let you have it on a sale or return basis, and then to stock up with about 25% more than you know you are likely to need. Don't forget, though, that as long as the host keeps serving drinks, the guests will keep drinking them, and if you want to finish at a specific time, it is best to say so on your invitation.

Getting the room ready
Getting the room ready for a drinks party usually takes at least an hour, by the time you have removed certain pieces of furniture and put your favourite ornaments out of harm's way. Try and leave as many chairs as you can, or a sofa or two for guests to flop on to. People traditionally stand at cocktail parties, but many guests may well wish to sit down after the first hour or so.
Put out as many ashtrays as you can muster—and cigarettes if you are feeling generous.

What to drink?
The dry martini is probably the most famous cocktail of all time, and correctly mixed, undoubtedly one of the finest. It is at its best made in small quantities, say enough for six or eight people. Anyone serving a martini at a cocktail party should mix it themselves thereby ensuring it is as fresh, cold and strong as possible for each guest. The following is a classic recipe:

Martini
8 parts dry gin
1 part dry vermouth
Place lumps of clean ice in a large mixing jug. Pour on the ingredients, stir quickly and serve immediately with the addition of an olive or small sliver of lemon peel in each glass.

Summer drinks parties are a wonderful opportunity to serve one' of the world's most famous drinks—Pimms No 1. It should be made exactly according to the instructions on the bottle, using good quality lemonade and served in glass mugs or tankards. On special occasions champagne may be added instead of lemonade—and the drink becomes a Pimms Royale.
Champagne or a good sparkling wine make an ideal cocktail party drink, as long as they are served at the correct temperature. To economize champagne may be added to orange juice in the following way to produce a

Buck's Fizz
1 part well chilled champagne
1 part fresh, canned or frozen orange juice
a little cognac or cointreau (optional)

A number of recipes for further cocktails and unusual mixed drinks appear on page 14. A good tip to remember when serving drinks at a cocktail party is to make the first one stronger than the last.

What to eat?
The object of offering one's guests food at a cocktail party is partly to absorb the effects of alcohol in an empty stomach and partly to enhance the flavour of the drinks being served. It is not therefore necessary to provide enormous snacks—in fact the criterion should be that whatever is being provided may be eaten in two mouthfuls. Flavours should be light and delicate, avoiding garlic, hot curry or very strong pâté if possible, and things that crumble or leave the hands messy. Offer roughly ten 'bits' per head from a selection of four to five items, in addition to the usual things like nuts and olives.

Egg and Caviar on Black Bread

☆☆ ① ①

Preparation and cooking time:
30 minutes
MAKES 32

6 eggs
8 slices of rye bread
about 2 oz. [4 tablespoons] **butter**
6 tablespoons mayonnaise (see page 62)
4 oz. Danish caviar [lumpfish roe]
To garnish:
sprigs of parsley

Hard-boil the eggs and cool. Remove the shells and thinly slice the eggs.
Cut four round shapes from each slice of rye bread, to make 32 shapes.
Spread with butter and place a slice of egg on each one. Place a small amount of mayonnaise in the middle of the egg and carefully put half a teaspoon of the caviar on top of each.
Garnish with small sprigs of parsley.

Cheese Sputniks

Preparation time:
45 minutes
MAKES enough for 20 people

4 large oranges
1½ lb. mild cheese
25 large black grapes
120 wooden cocktail sticks
25 stuffed green olives
25 walnut halves
6 oz. canned pineapple cubes
6 oz. canned mandarin oranges

Cut a thin slice from the base of the oranges to enable them to stand up.
Cut the cheese in ½-inch cubes and divide them into four piles.
Place a black grape on top of a cheese cube and gently pierce both with a cocktail stick. Stick this into one of the oranges, leaving enough showing so that people to remove it easily. Follow the same procedure with an olive on top of the cheese, then a walnut, a pineapple cube and so on until the oranges are thickly covered.

Variations:
Instead of an orange use a fresh pineapple, or a red or white cabbage.

Devils on Horseback

☆☆ ① ① 

Preparation and cooking time:
40 minutes
SERVES 8

16 large prunes
8 strips of bacon
8 anchovy fillets
16 blanched almonds
16 wooden cocktail sticks

Soak the prunes overnight in tea.
Heat oven to 400°F (Gas Mark 7, 200°C).
Simmer the prunes until tender, for 10-15 minutes. Drain, and when they are cool carefully remove the stones.
Remove the rind from the bacon and cut each strip in half. Flatten on a chopping-board.
Cut the anchovy fillets in half and wrap each half around a blanched almond. Place this inside a prune and wrap the bacon piece around the stuffed prune. Secure each with a cocktail stick, place on a baking tray and cook for 10-12 minutes.

Variations:
§ *Angels on horseback.* Use fresh or smoked oysters instead of the stuffed prunes, and cook as before.
§ Use small pieces of lamb's kidney instead of the stuffed prunes, and cook as before.

Taramasalata

 ① ① 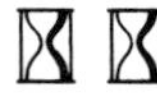

Preparation time:
30 minutes
MAKES 1½ lb.

8 oz. smoked cod's roe
6 slices of white bread
2 cloves of garlic
2 lemons
6 fl. oz. [¾ cup] **olive oil**
1 teaspoon paprika
4 oz. [½ cup] **butter**

With a sharp knife slice the cod's roe around the sides, and open flat. Scoop out the soft centre with a spoon.
Remove the crust from the bread and soak in water.
Crush the garlic and extract the juice from the lemons. Place the olive oil, garlic, lemon juice and paprika in the blender and mix for one minute.
Squeeze the bread to remove as much moisture as possible and add to the oil mixture. Blend for a further minute, then add the cod's roe, and mix again. Melt the butter and pour in to the mixture, and blend thoroughly with the rest.
Refrigerate for at least one hour before piping on to small slices of fried or toasted bread.

Smoked Salmon and Dill Rolls

☆ ① ① ①

Preparation time:
15 minutes
MAKES 16-20 rolls

4 large slices of smoked salmon
8 fl. oz. double [1 cup heavy] **cream**
dried dill weed
freshly ground black pepper
the juice of 1 lemon
about 20 wooden cocktail sticks

Stiffly beat the cream and add the dill weed to taste. Spread on to the smoked salmon slices, and sprinkle with pepper. Roll each slice up tightly and wrap in greaseproof or waxed paper. Place in the refrigerator for at least one hour before cutting into pieces.
Pierce each piece with a cocktail stick, and squeeze a little lemon juice over them all.

Ham and Cream Cheese Rolls

Preparation time:
10 minutes
MAKES 16-20 rolls

4 large slices of lean ham
6 oz. cream cheese
4 tablespoons chopped fresh chives
about 20 wooden cocktail sticks

Spread the ham with the cream cheese, sprinkle with chopped chives and roll up very tightly. Cut into pieces and secure each by piercing it with a cocktail stick.

opposite: top left: Devils on Horseback and Angels on Horseback
top right: Cheese Sputniks
below: Dips with crudités

Sausages in Chutney Sauce

Preparation and cooking time:
30 minutes
SERVES 16

2 lbs. small pork sausages
4 oz. [1 scant cup] **chopped almonds**
4 fl. oz. [½ cup] **chutney sauce**

Heat oven to 375°F (Gas Mark 5, 190°C).
Twist each sausage in half and cut at the new join, using kitchen scissors.
Bake for 20 minutes.
Strain off the fat, transfer to a serving dish, and pour the chutney sauce carefully over them.
Sprinkle with the chopped almonds and serve with cocktail sticks.

Beef and Horseradish Rolls

Preparation time:
10 minutes
MAKES 16 rolls

4 slices of medium rare cooked beef
4 fl. oz. double [½ cup heavy] **cream**
2 tablespoons horseradish sauce
16 wooden cocktail sticks

Whip the cream until stiff, and mix with the horseradish sauce. Spread on to the slices of beef, roll up, cut into pieces and serve each piece pierced with a cocktail stick.

Dips

These are always very popular at parties, are easily made, and can with very little effort be made to look extremely attractive. Almost any pâté or spread may be turned into a dip, by adding whipped cream, yoghurt, French dressing, thick mayonnaise or a soft cream cheese. The most important point to remember when making dips is to achieve a really thick consistency—for if they are at all runny, your guests as well as your carpets will be covered with messy dribbles. Serve dips with lots of small biscuits [crackers], crispbreads, potato crisps [chips]—and crudités composed of strips of raw carrot, celery sticks, raw cauliflower florets, scrubbed radishes, and so forth.

Pineapple and Cream Cheese Dip

Preparation time:
10 minutes
MAKES 6 oz.

6 oz. canned pineapple
4 oz. cream cheese
2 tablespoons tomato chutney or relish
4 tablespoons mayonnaise (see **page 62**)

Drain the pineapple and mash with a fork.
Mix the cream cheese with the tomato chutney and mayonnaise, add the mashed pineapple, and serve with small biscuits [crackers].

Green Cheese Dip

Preparation and cooking time:
10 minutes
MAKES 10 oz. [2 cups]

8 oz. Stilton or other blue veined cheese
10 fl. oz. double [1¼ cups heavy] **cream**
4 tablespoons chives, finely chopped

Mash the cheese in a small bowl with a fork, adding a little cream until a smooth consistency is obtained.
Beat the rest of the cream until it is fairly stiff, then stir it thoroughly into the cheese, with the chopped chives.

Smoked Cheese Dip

Preparation and cooking time:
10 minutes
SERVES 8

8 oz. smoked processed cheese
1 tablespoon prepared English mustard
2 tablespoons tomato ketchup
¼ teaspoon paprika
2-4 tablespoons double [heavy] **cream**
1 small onion
1 tablespoon capers

Grate the smoked cheese and mix with the mustard, tomato ketchup, and paprika. Add the cream until the right consistency is obtained.
Finely chop the onion and capers and mix these into the dip.

Curried Cheddar Dip

Preparation time:
10 minutes
MAKES 1 lb.

8 oz. [1 cup] **butter**
2 teaspoons curry powder
6 oz. Cheddar cheese
3 tablespoons mango chutney
2 oz. desiccated [½ cup shredded] **coconut**
5 fl. oz. double [½ cup heavy] **cream**

Cream the butter well with the curry powder and add the mango chutney. Grate the cheese. Whip the cream.
Mix together the butter, coconut and grated cheese, and fold in the whipped cream.

Cream Cheese Dip with Rosemary

Preparation time:
10 minutes
SERVES 6

6 oz. cream cheese
½ teaspoon powdered rosemary
8 fl. oz. [1 cup] **mayonnaise (see page 62)**
salt and pepper

Mix the cream cheese well with the powdered rosemary and add the mayonnaise.
Taste, and add the salt and pepper.
This dip is delicious sandwiched between two small cream crackers.

LUNCH & DINNER PARTIES

below: A welcoming atmosphere is created here by the open fire and soft warm candlelight, and by an informal and friendly tablesetting.

Giving a dinner party in your own home is one of the most enjoyable ways of entertaining. But unless you have great *sang-froid*, or a cheerfully relaxed disposition, a well-organized check-list will do wonders to keep you calm — and reassured that you have thought of everything at the appropriate moment. Prepare as much of the food as possible ahead of time; over-estimate how long it will take you to organise the room and so on, rather than find yourself having to rush through such preparations.

Making a welcome
It is the task of the hosts to do everything possible to make guests feel 'at home', which means creating an atmosphere that is warm and friendly, and one that shows you have taken time and effort. First impressions are important, so it is as well to think about the outside of the house. Make sure the entrance or porch is well lit, so that guests don't have to stumble around in the dark looking for the bell. Flowers and plants are a wonderful way of bringing the house to life, so make a big splash in the hall. Smaller arrangements, even a bunch of primroses in a wine glass, can be dotted around in strategic places. Use big paper flowers in pinks, magenta and orange clusters to augment your displays when the cost of fresh flowers is high, and don't forget even a few small bunches of strongly scented flowers like freesia, lily of the valley or mimosa can fill a room with a delicate fragrance if placed on a warm radiator or near a fire. (Scented candles can make an interesting and inexpensive alternative.) Arrange chairs and sofas in such a way that everyone can talk to each other without shouting. A semi-circle round the hearth with a low table in the middle for drinks, cigarettes and pre-dinner nibbles is an ideal way to break the ice and create an intimate cosy atmosphere.

What kind of party to give?
Giving a successful dinner party requires not only careful planning, but a keen awareness of one's own capabilities. Being overambitious is a pitfall that catches many inexperienced hosts, and it is always best to stick to what you know you can do best rather than what you think people will expect. Decide how many guests will fit comfortably round your dining table, and whether you can cope with cooking, serving and clearing away without outside help. Six to eight guests is about the maximum for a sit down dinner party where the host or hostess is doing all the work. Naturally if the party is very informal and restricted to close friends, numbers can be increased since everyone will be happy to lend a helping hand.

Timing
For a formal dinner party it is usual to ask guests to arrive half an hour before you intend to serve dinner, say 8.00 for 8.30 pm. Half to three quarters of an hour should be sufficient time for everyone to have at least two drinks and get to know each other.

Who sits where?
Traditionally the hostess sits at the top of the table with the host at the opposite end. It is accepted practice to put the senior male guest on the hostess' right, and the female guest of honour on the host's right. If there is no particular guest of honour, it is usual to choose someone who is either visiting the house for the first time, or a person whose position deserves special recognition. Foreign guests are often awarded the same privilege.

The menu
When planning the menu for a dinner party the most important consideration —as with any meal—must always be balance. With a rich main course involving a cream sauce, choose a pudding that is in direct contrast, something tart and fresh, and begin with a light appetizer. Experiment with different ways of preparing potatoes such as Lyonnaise, duchesse, puréed or plain boiled in their skins, then tossed in vinaigrette dressing. It is not necessary to stick always to the traditional three courses. Try dropping the appetizer and introducing a savoury like devilled soft roes, prunes wrapped in bacon or Welsh rarebit, or use salad as a course on its own or with cheese.
For small informal dinner parties in winter a huge bowl of shellfish soup or a giant casserole served with hot garlic bread or salad, and followed by cheese, are easy to prepare and serve. Try experimenting with a complete Chinese or Indian meal, or for that matter Russian or Mexican.

Serving the food and wine
For two people giving a dinner party without help, it is a good plan to have the first course ready on the table. The second course is usually taken round by the hostess, serving from the left of each guest, followed by the host with vegetables or sauces. Without help it is not necessary to serve the ladies first, which cuts down movement round the table and speeds up the whole operation.
It is quite acceptable for anyone managing without help to put the wine in the middle of the table for guests to help themselves, as long as the hosts keep an eye out for empty glasses. It is a nice, but by no means obligatory, touch to serve a glass of cold sherry or white wine with the first course, followed by red with the meat and maybe on special occasions a sweet wine or champagne with the dessert.

Coffee
These days the ladies almost *never* leave the gentlemen to their port and cigars! If guests are enjoying each other's company it seems a pity to break up the conversation, so unless the occasion is a particularly formal one, it is probably better to bring coffee and liqueurs to everyone round the table.

Port
If port is being served it should always be decanted and invariably tastes better accompanied by whatever nuts happen to be in season. Port is traditionally passed around the table—from right to left—by the guests themselves.
Bittermints, peppermint creams or crystallized ginger can be provided for those with a sweet tooth, and it is a nice gesture to make cigars and cigarettes available.

Leeks au Gratin

Preparation and cooking time:
40 minutes
SERVES 8

16 medium-sized leeks
8 spring onions [scallions]
salt and pepper
¼ teaspoon grated nutmeg
8 oz. [2⅔ cups] **toasted breadcrumbs**
6 oz. [¾ cup] **butter**
8 oz. [2 cups] **Gruyère** [Swiss] **cheese**

1

Spinach Flan
with Toasted Almonds

Liver Stroganoff
with boiled rice, and a salad of raw cauliflower and curly endive [chicory]

Ginger Ice-Cream

a powerful and robust red wine to match the main course, such as a Châteauneuf-du-Pape

2

Leeks au Gratin

Parsley Stuffed Pork Fillets
with Braised Red Cabbage and new potatoes

Lemon Mousse

a delicate red wine with plenty of character, such as Chianti Classico

3

Cucumber Ring
with Prawns and Apples

Kidneys in Wine Sauce
with boiled rice and mangetout [snow peas]

Black Cherry Tart

a red wine with plenty of body such as a good quality Spanish Rioja

4

Smoked Buckling Pâté

Lamb Chops
in Pastry Cases
with braised chicory and sauté potatoes

Caramel Topped Raspberries

a medium-dry wine with a slight sparkle, such as Vinho Verde: best served well-chilled

(see index for page numbers)

below: Smoked Buckling Pâté

Trim the leeks, leaving about 1-inch of green, wash them well and cook in boiling water for 10 minutes. Drain, and place in an ovenproof dish.
Clean, trim and finely chop the spring onions [scallions]. Sprinkle these over the leeks.
Dust with salt, pepper and the grated nutmeg.
Cover with the breadcrumbs and dot with butter.
Grate the cheese and sprinkle on top of the breadcrumbs.
Place under a preheated grill [broiler] for about 10 minutes until the cheese has melted and turned golden brown.
Serve at once.

Cucumber Ring with Prawns and Apples

Preparation and cooking time:
45 minutes
SERVES 8

3 large cucumbers
1 pint [2½ cups] **water**
a few sprigs of fresh mint
1½ oz. gelatine
1 medium-sized onion, chopped
1 tablespoon vinegar
a few drops of green colouring
salt and white pepper
2 apples
juice of 1 lemon
8 oz. fresh or defrosted shelled prawns or shrimp
For the aioli:
2 egg yolks
½ teaspoon salt
½ teaspoon sugar
½ teaspoon dry mustard
1½ tablespoons vinegar
8 fl. oz. [1 cup] **olive oil**
2 cloves of garlic, crushed
To garnish:
watercress sprigs
lemon slices

Peel, slice and cook the cucumber and mint in the water until tender. Cool, and discard the mint.
Soak the gelatine in 4 fl. oz. [½ cup] water for 5 minutes, before dissolving over low heat. Set aside to cool. Blend the cucumber and its liquid with the onion, put through a sieve and add the vinegar, the cool gelatine and a few drops of green colouring.
Season well with salt and pepper.
Pour in to a well-greased 1½-pint ring mould and refrigerate until set.
Peel and core the apples, cut them into small cubes, and dip them in lemon juice.
To make the aioli proceed as for making mayonnaise. Mix the egg yolks with the salt, sugar, mustard, 1 tablespoon of vinegar and the crushed garlic. Beat well and add the olive oil a little at a time, making sure it has been absorbed before adding more. When all the oil has been used up add the last of the vinegar.
Just before serving dip the mould in hot water for a moment and turn out on to a serving dish. Mix the prawns or shrimps with the apple cubes, coat with aioli, and place in the centre and around the mould.
Garnish with the watercress and lemon slices.

Smoked Buckling Pâté

Preparation and cooking time:
20 minutes
SERVES 8

8 large lemons
3 large buckling or kippers
8 tablespoons butter
2 teaspoons English mustard powder
freshly ground black pepper
12 fl. oz. double [1½ cups heavy] **cream**
To garnish:
parsley sprigs

Cut a thin slice from the stalk end of the lemons to enable them to stand upright. Cut the top off the other end, and remove the flesh with a grapefruit knife or teaspoon.
Carefully skin the buckling and remove the bones.
Melt the butter in a small saucepan.
Place the buckling in a blender with the melted butter, ¼ of the flesh and and juice from the lemons, the mustard and freshly ground pepper, and mix for a few seconds, or put the mixture through a food mill.
Beat the cream and fold in the buckling mixture. Pack into the lemon shells and refrigerate for about two hours.
Serve garnished with the parsley and offer hot toast.

Spinach Flan with Toasted Almonds

Preparation and cooking time:
1 hour
SERVES 8

8 oz. frozen chopped spinach
12 oz. shortcrust pastry (see page 61)
2 oz. [4 tablespoons] **butter**
1 large onion, finely chopped
6 large eggs
6 fl. oz. single [¾ cup light] **cream**
6 oz. [1½ cups] **Gruyère cheese, grated**
salt and pepper
¼ teaspoon nutmeg
To garnish:
4 oz. [1 cup] **blanched almonds**
½ oz. [1 tablespoon] **butter**

Heat oven to 400°F (Gas Mark 6, 200°C).
Defrost and drain the spinach.
Line a 12-inch flan ring with the pastry, prick the bottom well, and bake blind for 10 minutes. Remove the flan, and reduce the heat to 375°F (Gas Mark 5, 190°C).
Meanwhile melt the butter in a saucepan and sauté the onion for 3 minutes, then add the spinach and heat gently for 5 minutes. Remove from the stove.
Beat the eggs, add the cream and 4 ounces [1 cup] of the grated cheese. Mix this with the spinach. Season with salt, pepper and nutmeg.
Pour into the flan case and top with the remaining cheese.
Bake in the oven for 20 minutes, or until the filling has set.
Sauté the almonds in ½ oz. [1 tablespoon] butter until they are evenly browned. Scatter them over the flan before serving.

Kidneys in Wine Sauce

 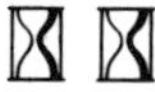

Preparation and cooking time:
1 hour
SERVES 8

16 lamb's kidneys
8 tablespoons flour
2 large onions

2 oz. [4 tablespoons] **butter**
4 tablespoons chopped parsley
2 large cloves garlic
10 fl. oz. [$1\frac{1}{4}$ cups] **red wine**
10 fl. oz. single [$1\frac{1}{4}$ cups light] **cream**

Skin the kidneys, cut them in half and remove the cores. Dust with flour.
Finely chop the onions.
Melt the butter in a frying-pan, add the kidneys and sauté quickly until they are brown. Now add the chopped onions and fry with the kidneys for a further 5 minutes.
Add 3 tablespoons of the chopped parsley, crush the garlic and add, with the wine to the kidneys.
Reduce the heat and simmer for 35-40 minutes.
Remove the pan from the heat and stir in the cream. Reheat gently, but do not boil.
Garnish with the rest of the parsley and serve with rice.

Lamb Chops in Pastry Cases

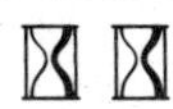

Preparation and cooking time:
1 hour
SERVES 8

8 lamb chump chops
4 oz. [$\frac{1}{2}$ cup] **butter**
2 large onions
8 oz. button mushrooms
8 sprigs of fresh rosemary
salt and pepper
1 lb. puff pastry (see page 61)
2 eggs, lightly beaten

Heat oven to 450°F (Gas Mark 8, 230°C).
Trim excess fat from the chops and brown them quickly in 2 oz. [4 tablespoons] of the butter. Remove from the pan and set them aside to cool.
Finely chop the onion and the mushrooms.
Melt the rest of the butter, and sauté the onions and mushrooms for a few minutes.
Season well with salt and pepper, remove from the heat and allow to cool.
Roll out the pastry and cut 8 pieces, large enough to encase each chop. Place a chop in the middle of a piece of pastry, spread a spoonful of the onion and mushroom mixture on top and add a sprig of rosemary. Season with salt and pepper.
Moisten the edges of the pastry with the beaten egg and wrap the pastry carefully over the filling and press the edges firmly together.
Place on a baking sheet, pastry-join down and brush the surface with egg.
Bake in the oven for 15-20 minutes, until the pastry is golden brown.

Parsley Stuffed Pork Fillets

Preparation and cooking time:
2 hours
SERVES 8

4 x 1 lb. fillets of pork
8 tablespoons of chopped parsley
salt and pepper
4 oz. [$\frac{1}{2}$ cup] **butter**
$1\frac{1}{2}$ pint [$3\frac{3}{4}$ cups] **stock or water**
4 tablespoons cornflour [cornstarch]
To garnish:
chopped parsley

Trim the fillets of excess fat and remove the sinews. Cut the fillets halfway through lengthwise, and flatten them with a meat-hammer. Place the fillets side by side, so that they just over-lap.
Arrange the parsley thickly down the centre of the meat and season well with salt and pepper.
Carefully roll up the meat like a Swiss [jelly] roll, and secure with several pieces of fine string.
Heat the butter in a large frying-pan and sauté the meat until it is brown on all sides.
Pour over the stock or water and bring it to the boil. Reduce the heat and cook gently, covered, for 30-40 minutes.
Remove the meat from the stock and keep hot.
Mix the cornflour [cornstarch] with a little cold water and add it to the hot meat stock.
Bring to the boil, stirring constantly until the gravy has thickened.
Season well with salt and pepper.
Slice the meat, being careful to discard all the string. Place on a hot serving-dish, pour the gravy over and sprinkle with a little chopped parsley.
Serve with sweet potatoes and red cabbage.

Braised Red Cabbage

Preparation and cooking time:
$1\frac{1}{2}$ hours
SERVES 8

1 large red cabbage
4 oz. [$\frac{1}{2}$ cup] **butter**
2 tablespoons sugar
3 tablespoons cider vinegar
3 tablespoons redcurrant jelly
6 tablespoons water
3 medium-sized cooking apples
salt and pepper

Remove the outer leaves from the cabbage, cut it in quarters and remove the stalk. Finely shred the cabbage.
Melt the butter in a heavy saucepan, and stir in the sugar, taking care not to brown. Add the cabbage, vinegar, redcurrant jelly and the water.
Peel, core and slice the apples and add to the saucepan. Stir well and simmer, covered, for 1 hour. Stir occasionally and if necessary add a little more water.
Serve with the pork tenderloin. It is also excellent with goose or duck.

Liver Stroganoff

Preparation and cooking time:
40 minutes
SERVES 8

$2\frac{1}{2}$ lbs. calves or lamb's liver
2 large onions
8 oz. button mushrooms
4 oz. [$\frac{1}{2}$ cup] **butter**
salt and freshly ground pepper
8 fl. oz. single [1 cup light] **cream**
4 tablespoons chopped parsley

Cut the liver into strips about $\frac{1}{2}$-inch wide and $1\frac{1}{2}$-inches long.
Slice the onion.
Wipe clean the mushrooms and slice them.
Melt half the butter in a frying-pan, add the onions and fry gently until golden.
Add the mushrooms and sauté for a few minutes with the onions.
Remove the onions and mushrooms from the pan and keep warm.
Add the rest of the butter to the pan and heat until it begins to foam.

above: Kidneys in Wine Sauce
left: Black Cherry Tart

Put in the sliced liver and fry quickly for 3-4 minutes until it is light brown on all sides.
Return the mushrooms and onions to the pan, season with salt and pepper, stir in the cream and cook for a further minute.
Sprinkle with chopped fresh parsley and serve on a bed of rice.

Ginger Ice-Cream

Preparation and cooking time:
25 minutes plus freezing time
SERVES 8

16 fl. oz. [2 cups] **milk**
2 whole eggs
4 egg yolks
8 oz. castor [1 cup fine] **sugar**
1 teaspoon vanilla essence
16 fl. oz. double [2 cups heavy] **cream**
3 large pieces of preserved ginger
For the sauce:
1 pint [2½ cups] **water**
2 tablespoons cornflour [cornstarch]
7 fl. oz. [⅞ cup] **white wine**
6 tablespoons preserved ginger, finely chopped

Bring the milk almost to the boil.
Beat the whole eggs and the egg yolks together with the sugar until the mixture is light and fluffy.
Stir in the milk and strain the mixture back into the saucepan. Heat very slowly, stirring constantly, until it just coats the back of the spoon. Add the vanilla essence and set aside to cool. Pour the cold custard in to a foil container and freeze until it has just become firm.
Remove from the container and beat well.
Whip the cream and finely chop the stem ginger. Fold into the ice cream and replace in the freezer compartment of the refrigerator.
When slightly firm beat up the ice cream once more, then freeze until completely firm.
Meanwhile, make the sauce. Blend a little of the water with the cornflour [cornstarch] until smooth, and then stir in the rest of the water.
Bring slowly to the boil, stirring constantly, and add the wine and chopped ginger. Remove from the heat and cool.
Serve the ice cream with the sauce.

Caramel Topped Raspberries

Preparation and cooking time:
30 minutes
SERVES 8

1 lb. unsweetened frozen raspberries
8 macaroons
8 teaspoons brandy
10 fl. oz. double [1¼ cups heavy] **cream**
6 oz. [1 cup] **brown sugar**

Defrost the raspberries and drain away the juice.
Place the macaroons in 8 individual ovenproof dishes and pour over the brandy.
Spoon on the drained raspberries and press down lightly with a teaspoon.
Top each with the cream and sprinkle with plenty of brown sugar.
Place under a hot grill [broiler] until the sugar has melted and serve at once.

Variations:
Use any other canned, purèed or frozen fruit instead of raspberries, but keep in mind that the cream and sugar topping is very sweet, so it is best suited to fruit with a slightly sharp taste, like blackcurrants or gooseberries.

Black Cherry Tart

Preparation and cooking time:
45 minutes
SERVES 8

12 oz. rich shortcrust pastry (see page 61)
1 lb. canned stoned black cherries
1 oz. gelatine
4 tablespoons brandy
8 fl. oz. double [1 cup heavy] **cream**

Heat oven to 400°F (Gas Mark 6, 200°C).
Roll out the pastry and line a well buttered 12-inch fluted flan case.
Bake blind for 20-25 minutes, then take out and cool on a wire rack.
Drain the cherries and reserve the juice.
Soak the gelatine for 5 minutes in the cherry juice before dissolving over a low heat. Set aside to cool and then mix with the brandy.
Beat the cream until stiff and spoon on to the bottom of the cold pastry case, reserving a little of the cream for decoration. Neatly arrange the cherries on top.
Brush the cherries with the almost set juice.
Decorate with rosettes of whipped cream.

Variation:
Instead of lining a flan tin with the pastry, roll it out into a 10- or 12-inch circle and scallop the edge with a fluted cutter. (Press down only half the cutter to make an edge of semi-circles.) Prick the surface thoroughly before baking and then arrange the filling in the centre.
In this case, the consistency of the filling is very important—it must be thick enough to hold its shape without running.

Lemon Mousse

Preparation and cooking time:
30 minutes
SERVES 8

1 oz. gelatine
4 fl. oz. [½ cup] **water**
3 large lemons
6 eggs
8 tablespoons castor [fine] **sugar**
To decorate:
lemon slices
6 fl. oz. double [¾ cup heavy] **cream, whipped**

Soak the gelatine in the water for 5 minutes before dissolving over low heat. Set aside to cool.
Finely grate the zest of the lemons and squeeze out the juice.
Separate the eggs. Cream the yolks with the sugar until very light and fluffy.
When the gelatine is cool mix with the yolks, and add the lemon juice and the grated zest. Stir well and set aside.
Whisk the egg whites until stiff.
As soon as the yolk mixture begins to set, fold it very gently in to the egg whites.
Refrigerate for at least 3 hours.
Decorate with the whipped cream and the slices of lemon before serving.

BUFFET PARTIES

The buffet, be it lunch or dinner, has several advantages over a more formal round-the-table dinner party. The atmosphere will be a more relaxed and informal one, with your friends circulating freely—and it is possible to invite many more people. Serving an imaginative, well presented buffet party is one of the easiest and most rewarding ways of entertaining.

How many people
The number of people it is possible to invite is dictated by the size of the room in which it is intended to hold the party. It is obviously

below: Arrange the food and wine for easy access, and in logical sequence—as here, around a circular table.

possible to invite more people if a separate dining room is available from which to serve the food. Chairs or cushions should be arranged in groups so that guests can sit comfortably together, and there should be sufficient table space beside each group on which they can safely place their glasses and used plates.

Layout of the table
Where you site the serving table is important. If the room is large enough this may be in the centre, so that guests can help themselves from all four sides. If not, set the table to one side leaving enough room, if necessary, for someone to serve from behind. The table should ideally be long and narrow, and covered with a white or coloured tablecloth to the floor, with the corners pinned up (inside) so people won't trip over them. (If you haven't a large enough cloth a sheet will do—protect the table-top with a spill-proof layer first.) It is best to lay out the table in a logical order, to avoid confusion and congestion. If someone is serving, put plates and cutlery on the right, main dishes in the centre, fruit, cheese, wine and glasses on the left. If your friends are helping themselves lay plates, knives, forks and napkins along the front edge of the table, with the food behind. If possible wine and glasses should be kept on a separate table in a different corner of the room. If there's space another small table—even a well-covered card table—will be useful for stacking used plates.

What to eat?
There are no hard and fast rules about what may be served at a buffet supper; the only criterion is that the food should be easy to eat with a fork. The key to a successful buffet is simplicity and impeccable presentation. It is usual to offer two main dishes, one hot and one cold. Since everyone will not necessarily be eating at the same time, the hot dish will have to be kept warm, (with a hot plate or candle-warmer) or made up in smaller dishes to be served in relay. Serve a selection of green or rice based salads which go equally well with either dish. Starters may be dropped altogether or kept very simple. Finish off with one good dessert, a selection of cheeses, fresh fruit and coffee.

The host's responsibility
The main responsibility of the host is to see that everyone has enough to eat and drink and that dirty plates and glasses are not allowed to pile up in unsightly heaps. Once the party is under way it is a practical idea to give each group of guests its own bottle of wine.

New England Clam Chowder

☆☆ ①①① ⌛

Preparation and cooking time:
40 minutes
SERVES 8

3 x 8 oz. canned minced clams
1 lb. canned baby clams
2 medium-sized onions
2 oz. [4 tablespoons] **butter**
1 pint [2½ cups] **water**
4 large potatoes
½ teaspoon Worcestershire sauce
10 fl. oz. [1¼ cups] **milk**
salt and pepper
10 fl. oz. double [1¼ cups heavy] **cream**

Strain the juice from the cans of clams and reserve.
Slice the onions and sauté in butter until soft and transparent. Set aside.
Peel the potatoes. Thinly slice two of the potatoes and cook in the clam juice until tender, then mash them in to the clam juice.
Parboil the other potatoes, cut into small cubes, and add to the clam juice mixture.
Put in the Worcestershire sauce.
Add the milk and onions and gently simmer for 5-7 minutes. Now add the clams, and salt and pepper to taste. Cook for 2 minutes over a low heat. Remove the pan from the stove and gradually stir in the cream.
Return the pan to a low heat and cook until the cream is warmed. Do not let mixture come to the boil.
Serve immediately.

Herring Table

Herrings are among the most popular items on the Scandinavian smorgasbord. Most good delicatessen shops stock either salted herrings, or herrings in brine. These should always be soaked in water for 6-8 hours before using. The matjes herring is probably the best known abroad. It is sometimes sold by weight but more often in cans. Unlike the other varieties this herring need not be

1

Herring Table

Boeuf en Croûte
with a curly endive [chicory] and walnut salad, and a potato salad with chopped chives

Pear Delight

a good full-bodied Burgundy to match the rich main course, such as Gevrey Chambertin

2

Smoked Mackerel Pâté

Chicken Salad
with Mango and Melon
with a boiled rice and nut salad, a tomato salad, and a plain green salad

Hazelnut Meringue Cake

an inexpensive fresh and flowery Moselle to be drunk through the meal, such as Bernkasteler Riesling

3

Asparagus Mousse

Penthouse Pie
with a watercress and celery salad

Apricot Cake

a fresh young fruity wine, such as Beaujolais nouveau: best served slightly chilled

4

New England Clam Chowder

Tandoori Chicken Pieces
with jacket potatoes and a beetroot salad

Pruneau Millefeuille

a light well-flavoured white wine such as an Italian Soave: best served chilled

(see index for page numbers)

soaked before use, and could be substituted for salted herrings if desired.

Marinated Smoked Buckling

✡  

Preparation and cooking time: *30 minutes*
SERVES 12

12 smoked buckling or kippers
For the marinade:
6 tablespoons tomato purée
6 tablespoons vinegar
6 tablespoons olive oil
6 tablespoons water
3 bayleaves
1½ teaspoons salt
freshly ground black pepper
3 teaspoons sugar
For the garnish:
6 tablespoons chopped chives

Remove the head, skin and bones from the bucklings and arrange them in strips on a serving dish.
In a screw-top jar put together the ingredients for the marinade and shake well. Pour the mixture over the smoked buckling fillets, and leave covered in a cool place for 1-2 hours.
Sprinkle with the chopped chives before serving.

Piquant Herring

Preparation and cooking time: *30 minutes*
SERVES 12

6 large matjes herrings
6 hardboiled eggs
6 large, red tomatoes
For the sauce:
3 tablespoons made English mustard
3 tablespoons sugar
6 tablespoons wine vinegar
6 fl. oz. [¾ cup] **olive oil**
3 large sweet pickled gherkin
For the garnish:
chopped fresh dill or parsley

Cut the matjes herrings in half and roll each half up. Place these in the middle of a serving dish.
Cut the eggs and tomatoes into wedges and place around the herrings.
Mix together the mustard, sugar and vinegar, and beat well. Add the oil, little by little, as for mayonnaise.
Finely chop the gherkins and add it to the sauce.
Pour over the herrings and garnish with the dill or parsley.
Serve very cold.

Soused Herrings

✡  

Preparation and cooking time: *2 hours*
SERVES 12

12 fresh herrings
6 fl. oz. [¾ cup] **milk**
12 tablespoons oatmeal
4 oz. [8 tablespoons] **butter**
salt and freshly ground pepper
For the marinade:
1 pint [2½ cups] **wine vinegar**
10 fl. oz. [1¼ cups] **water**
12 oz. [1½ cups] **sugar**
6 bayleaves
4 cloves
For the garnish:
sprigs of fresh dill
1 small onion, finely chopped

Clean the herrings, remove the heads and trim the fins and tails. Wash them and drain well. Dip in the milk and coat with oatmeal. Season with salt and pepper.
Heat the butter in a large frying-pan and fry the herrings until they are golden brown on both sides. Remove

left: Smoked Mackerel Pâté
above: Hazelnut Meringue Cake
right: Chicken Salad with Mango and Melon

them from the frying-pan and set aside to cool.
Put all the ingredients for the marinade in to a saucepan and heat until the sugar has dissolved. Remove from the heat and cool.
Pour the cold marinade over the fish and garnish with the dill sprigs and the chopped onion.

Herrings in Sherry

Preparation and cooking time:
30 minutes
SERVES 12

6 matjes herrings
6 tablespoons sugar
8 tablespoons water
6 fl. oz. [$\frac{3}{4}$ cup] **sherry**
4 tablespoons wine vinegar
2 medium-sized onions
8 crushed white peppercorns
fresh sprigs of dill

Cut the herrings crosswise into 1-inch wide strips and place them on a serving dish.
Dissolve the sugar in the water before adding the sherry and the vinegar. Leave to cool.
Slice the onions, separate into rings and place over the fish with the crushed peppercorns. Pour the cold marinade over and refrigerate for 2-3 hours before serving.
Garnish with the sprigs of dill.

Smoked Mackerel Pâté

Preparation and cooking time:
30 minutes
SERVES 12

4 large smoked mackerel
8 oz. [1 cup] **butter**
6 tablespoons horseradish sauce
4 lemons
8 slices of white bread
salt and pepper
To garnish:
parsley sprigs
slices of lemon

Carefully skin and remove the bones from the mackerel.
Melt the butter, squeeze the lemons.
Remove the crust from the bread and soak the bread in water for a few minutes. Take out and squeeze dry.
Mix together the damp bread, melted butter, horseradish sauce and the lemon juice with a little salt and a generous amount of freshly ground pepper.
Break up the mackerel flesh with a fork, and add it to the bread mixture.
Blend thoroughly and spoon into a serving dish.
Refrigerate for at least 2 hours.
Garnish with the parsley sprigs and lemon slices and serve with hot toast.

Asparagus Mousse

Preparation and cooking time:
45 minutes
SERVES 12

1 lb. canned asparagus spears
$1\frac{1}{2}$ oz. gelatine
6 eggs
$\frac{1}{2}$ teaspoon salt
freshly ground white pepper
1 tablespoon sugar
2 tablespoons dry mustard
6 tablespoons tarragon vinegar
6 drops of green colouring
16 fl. oz. double [2 cups heavy] **cream**

To garnish
4 fl. oz. [¼ cup] **made up aspic jelly**
8 slices of lemon

Drain the liquid from the asparagus and soak the gelatine in this for 5 minutes before dissolving over a low heat. Set aside to cool.
Beat together the eggs, salt, pepper, sugar and mustard.
Bring the vinegar to the boil and remove from the heat. Add the egg mixture and stir well. Return to a low heat, stirring constantly, until the mixture has thickened.
Remove from the heat again. Add the cool gelatine and the green colouring.
Lightly whip the cream and fold into the egg mixture with the asparagus spears reserving a few for garnish.
Pour into a dish and refrigerate for half an hour.
Make up the aspic jelly and glaze the cold mousse with this.
Arrange the remaining asparagus spears and the slices of lemons in the jelly.
Carefully place the mousse in the refrigerator taking care not to spoil the pattern.
Chill for 1 hour or until set.
Serve with buttered brown bread.

Boeuf en Croûte

Fillet of beef in a pastry case

 ① ① ①

Preparation and cooking time:
2 hours
SERVES 12

1 x 4½ lbs. fillet of beef
freshly ground pepper
3 oz. [6 tablespoons] **butter**
8 oz. button mushrooms
4 tablespoons chopped parsley
½ teaspoon salt
6 oz. good quality liver pâté
12 oz. puff pastry, (see page 61)
1 egg, beaten

Heat oven to 400°F (Gas Mark 6, 200°C).
Trim off all the excess fat and sinew from the meat. Roll into a neat bolster and tie with fine string at intervals to secure the shape. Dust with pepper.
Heat the butter in a frying-pan and brown the meat all over.
Transfer the beef to a roasting tin and roast in the oven for 10 minutes.
Take out and leave to cool. Remove the string.
Wipe clean and slice the mushrooms, and sauté in the butter left from the meat, mix with the parsley and a little salt and leave to cool.
Roll out the pastry to a rectangle about ⅛-inch thick, and large enough to easily cover the meat.
Spread the pâté and the mushrooms over the top and sides of the fillet, and place it, pâté side down, in the centre of the pastry. Then spread pâté on the remaining side.
Beat the egg and brush along the edges of the pastry, and fold the pastry over the meat, pressing the two sides firmly together. Brush the pastry ends with egg and fold up, cutting away any surplus pastry. Use this for making decorative leaves.
Place the *Boeuf en Croûte* on a baking tray, pastry join down, brush with egg, and place the pastry leaves in the centre of the pastry. Brush again.
Bake in the centre of the oven for 30-40 minutes until the pastry is golden brown.
Serve hot or cold.

Tandoori Chicken Pieces

① 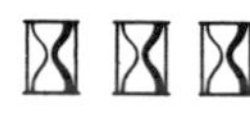

Preparation and cooking time:
45 minutes, plus 4 hours marinating time
SERVES 12

3 x 2½ lb. chickens
salt and pepper
10 fl. oz. [1¼ cups] **plain yoghurt**
1 teaspoon hot chilli powder
3 cloves of garlic, crushed
¼ teaspoon ground ginger
¼ teaspoon ground coriander
1 teaspoon mild curry powder
juice of 1 lemon
3 oz. [6 tablespoons] **butter**
6 tablespoons sugar

Heat oven to 375°F, (Gas Mark 5, 190°C).
Joint the chickens and wipe them dry. Season with salt and pepper.
Make the marinade by mixing the yoghurt, chilli powder, garlic cloves, ginger, coriander, curry powder and the lemon juice. Mix well and marinate the chicken joints in this for 4 hours, turning several times.
Melt the butter and the sugar in a frying-pan, and fry the chicken pieces until they are brown on all sides.
Wrap each chicken piece in foil and cook in the oven for 20 minutes.
Heat the marinade and serve with the chicken, baked potatoes and beetroot [beet] salad.

Chicken Salad

with melon and mango dressing

①

Preparation and cooking time:
1½ hours
SERVES 12

2 x 3½ lb. chickens
1 onion, sliced
2 carrots, scraped and sliced
1 bouquet garni
½ teaspoon salt
For the dressing:
1 pint [2½ cups] **mayonnaise** (see **page 62**)
10 fl. oz. double [1¼ cups heavy] **cream**
8 tablespoons mango chutney
To garnish:
1 Honeydew or 2 Charantais melons
2 red peppers

In a large saucepan cover the chickens with water, add the onion, carrots, bouquet garni and the salt. Bring to the boil, reduce the heat and simmer for 40 minutes. Take off the heat and leave the chicken to cool in the liquid.
When they are cold, take them out of the saucepan, remove the skin and pull the meat off the bones. Place the meat in a neat row on a large serving-dish.
Cut the melon into narrow boat-shaped pieces and remove the pips and the rind. Arrange on the serving-dish with the chicken.
Whip the cream and mix with the mayonnaise. Add the mango chutney and season with salt and pepper.
Wash the peppers, remove the cores and the seeds. Slice them into rings.
Spoon the dressing over the chicken and the melon, and garnish with the pepper rings.
Serve with a rice and nut salad, a tomato salad and a plain green salad.

Penthouse Pie

① 

Preparation and cooking time:
1½ hours
SERVES 12

2 medium-sized onions
3 green peppers
8 oz. button mushrooms
1 beef stock cube
2½ fl. oz. canned tomato purée
2 oz. [4 tablespoons] **butter**
½ bottle red wine
3½ lb. lean minced [ground] **beef**

salt and pepper
3 lb. cooked mashed potatoes

Heat oven to 375°F (Gas Mark 5, 190°C).
Slice the onions, wash and remove the cores and the seeds from the peppers, and slice them into rings.
Wipe clean the mushrooms and slice them thinly.
Dissolve the stock cube in 5 fl. oz. [$\frac{5}{8}$ cup] of boiling water.
Melt the butter in a large saucepan. Add the onions and fry gently for a few minutes, then add the peppers and the mushrooms and sauté for a further few minutes.
Add the tomato purée, mix well and then add the minced [ground] beef. Break up the meat with a fork and stir to mix with the mushrooms, onions and the purée.
Pour in the stock and the wine and adjust the seasoning.
Transfer to a heat-proof dish and pipe the mashed potatoes on the top.
Bake in the oven for 30 minutes, then increase the heat to 450°F (Gas Mark 8, 230°C) for 10 minutes or until the pie is well-browned.
Serve with a watercress and celery salad.

Apricot Flan

Preparation and cooking time:
1 hour
SERVES 12

12 oz. rich shortcrust pastry (see page 61)
1 lb. canned apricot halves
8 oz. apricot jam
4 oz. [$\frac{1}{2}$ cup] **chopped almonds**
6 fl. oz. double [$\frac{3}{4}$ cup heavy] **cream, whipped**

Heat oven to 400°F (Gas Mark 6, 200°C).
Make the pastry and roll out to a round $\frac{1}{4}$-inch thick. Prick all over with a fork, and bake blind for 20 minutes. When golden brown take out and cool on a wire rack.
Drain the apricots thoroughly.
Melt the jam gently over low heat.
Brush the cold pastry with a thin layer of this, arrange the apricots neatly on top and sprinkle with the chopped almonds. Glaze with a thick layer of the apricot jam.
Decorate with rosettes of whipped cream.

Pear Delight

Cooking and preparation time:
$\frac{1}{2}$ hour
SERVES 12

24 large canned pear halves
8 oz. walnut halves
6 oz. cream cheese
1 pint double [$2\frac{1}{2}$ cups heavy] **cream**
8 drops of green colouring

Drain the pears. Chop the walnuts, reserving 12 halves for decoration.
Soften the cream cheese with a little of the juice from the pears.
Whip the cream and add the colouring. Mix half of the cream with the cheese and chopped walnuts.
Spoon the mixture into the hollows of the pears and sandwich the two halves together to reform the original shape.
Decorate with the rest of the cream piped along the join of the pears and place half a walnut on top of each.

Pruneau Millefeuille

Puff pastry slice with prunes

Preparation and cooking time:
$1\frac{1}{2}$ hours
SERVES 10

12 oz. puff pastry (see page 61)
1 lb. large prunes, soaked in tea overnight
16 fl. oz. double [2 cups heavy] **cream**
4 tablespoons castor [fine] **sugar**
2 teaspoons vanilla essence
For the icing:
6 oz. icing [$1\frac{1}{2}$ cups confectioners'] **sugar**
3 tablespoons boiling water

Heat oven to 450°F (Gas Mark 8, 225°C).
Cook the prunes for 10-15 minutes. Strain and allow to cool. Remove the stones and put the prunes through a strainer, using a wooden spoon to press the pulp through.
Roll out the pastry to a rectangle 5-inches by 20-inches and cut into 2 rectangles 5-inches by 10-inches. Prick well with a fork. Place on a well greased and floured baking sheet and bake blind for 25 minutes until the pastry is golden brown. Take out and cool.
Whip the cream, add the sugar and the vanilla essence. Reserve a little of this for decoration and fold the puréed prunes into the rest of the cream.
Spoon the prune cream onto one of the pastry rectangles, placing the other on top.
Mix the icing and spread it on top.
Decorate with the reserved cream.

Hazelnut Meringue Cake

Preparation and cooking time:
1 hour 15 minutes
SERVES 10

6 oz. [1 cup] **shelled hazelnuts**
4 egg whites
8 oz. [1 cup fine] **castor sugar**
1 teaspoon vanilla essence
$\frac{1}{2}$ teaspoon vinegar
14 oz. canned blackcurrants, strained
16 fl. oz. double [2 cups heavy] **cream**
4 tablespoons icing [confectioners'] **sugar**

Heat oven to 370°F (Gas Mark 5, 190°C).
Place the hazelnuts in a baking tin and brown in the oven. Remove, and allow to cool. Rub the nuts well to remove the outer skin. Crush the kernels with a rolling pin or put them through a mincer [grinder].
Rub the sides of two 9-inch sandwich tins with butter, dust with flour and line the bottom with waxed or grease-proof paper.
Whisk the egg whites until stiff, and then gradually beat in half of the castor sugar. Continue to beat until the egg whites are very stiff, adding the vanilla essence and the vinegar. Lastly fold in the rest of the sugar and the minced hazelnuts.
Fill the prepared tins equally and bake in the oven for 35-45 minutes. Take them out and carefully remove from the tins. Cool on a wire rack.
Drain the juice from the blackcurrants.
Whip the cream and reserve half for decoration. Fold the blackcurrants into the other half and spoon on to one of the cakes, placing the other on top.
Dust the top of the cake with icing [confectioners'] sugar and decorate with rosettes, made from the reserved cream.

WINE & CHEESE PARTIES

The wine and cheese party is an amusing and inexpensive way of entertaining, and is a particularly good way to entertain large numbers of people—especially for cooks who do not have the time to make elaborate preparations. But while the basic ingredients for the party are on the face of it simple to prepare, a wine and cheese party can be a dreary affair if attention is not given to presentation and detail. Simply to hack up a piece of Cheddar, open a few bottles of cheap wine and hope for the best is not enough. Cheese is something that requires other textures and flavours around it, if it is to be the main food of the evening.

What kinds of cheese
In order to achieve variety at least six cheeses—more if pocket and availability allow—should be offered. Contrast soft and hard—a rich creamy cheese such as Boursin with a strong blue Stilton or Roquefort, and the delicious smoked cheeses from Austria. Set off the nutty taste of good Cheddar against the soft rich flavour of Brie or Camembert. Try to locate a goat's or sheep's milk cheese. Dolcelatte, a milder edition of Gorgonzola, is one of the best Italian cheeses, with a full creamy texture when at its peak.
Certain cheeses need careful handling to ensure they arrive on the table in perfect condition. A ripe Brie, for example, will quickly lose its delicate aroma and texture if refrigerated, so if possible warn your grocer well in advance and collect the softer cheeses on the afternoon of the party.
Even if you have a good variety of cheeses, an exclusive diet of them could become monotonous, so it is as well to prepare one or two dips which have a strong spicy originality of their own, and can be eaten with crudités: fresh crisp raw vegetables like celery, cucumber, green pepper or carrot. The crudités can act as a centrepiece to the table, and can look quite spectacular. Their clean cool taste makes a welcome refreshment in the warm bustle of the party. The dips themselves should be of a fairly thick consistency or they may dribble messily on clothes or carpets.

How much to buy
Judging the correct quantity of cheese to buy for your party is not easy, and the tendency is usually to overestimate your friends' appetites. Bread and cheese is filling, so allow not more than four ounces per person, with a higher proportion of the soft runny cheeses, like Brie, than of the hard Cheddar-types.

What kind of bread
Crisp loaves of French bread are the traditional accompaniment for cheese, but it is more interesting if you can offer a choice of wholemeal, rye, oatcakes, crispbreads and water biscuits [crackers]. Hot garlic bread could be added, to eat separately.

What else
If you feel that cheese and its accompaniments are not varied enough, include a selection of home made pâtés which can be prepared two or three days in advance, or a huge bowl of watercress or crisp lettuce (in bite-sized pieces) with a vinaigrette dressing —plus forks. Fruit is perfect with or after cheese, so make up several bowls of apples—and, if they are in season, pears and fresh figs.

What to drink
Make sure there is an adequate supply of both red and white wine. A half to three quarters of a bottle per head should last the evening, but it is a good idea to buy on a sale or return basis, and to add an extra 25% to keep in reserve. Nowadays it is usually possible to buy cheap but sound wine in gallon jars or two litre bottles. Try a sample well before the party to make sure of the quality. It would be thoughtful to have a bottle of Scotch handy for older guests who may like something stronger than wine during the course of the evening, and don't forget that both cider and beer go well with almost all kinds of cheese.

Creating an atmosphere
Wine and cheese parties are informal affairs where everyone helps themselves to food and drink when they feel like it. It is best to set the food out, buffet style, with colourful paper plates and plenty of napkins. Cheeses can be arranged on straw matting or wooden chopping boards. If food is laid out in advance, make sure that it is kept fresh by covering it with a damp cloth right up until the last moment.
Laying out the food should, however, be left to the last minute so that it all looks as fresh and appetising as possible. Add little bowls of green and black olives or quartered radishes for guests to nibble as they go round the table, and make sure there is plenty of sea salt, black pepper and quarters of lemon for the raw vegetables.
Candlelight is always more flattering than electricity, but make sure that guests can see what they are doing. Use thick candles in groups of three or four to create a soft overall effect, but concentrated where light is needed. Candles, yellow and white make a good combination, may be decorated round the base with flowers of the same colour, or hide a low watt bulb behind large arrangements of leaves to throw a warm dappled effect on the walls and ceiling.

Cheese-Stuffed Celery

Preparation time:
20 minutes
MAKES about 50

10 celery stalks
12 oz. cream cheese
3 tablespoons chives, finely chopped
4 drops tabasco
salt and pepper

Wash the celery, discard the leaves and cut into 2-inch pieces.
Mix the cheese with the chives and tabasco. Season with a little salt and pepper.
Using a piping bag with a fluted nozzle pipe the cheese into the hollow of the celery pieces.

Cream Cheese and Salami Dip

Preparation time:
15 minutes
MAKES about 1 lb.

1 medium-sized onion
4 oz. thinly sliced salami
8 oz. cream cheese
6 fl. oz. [¾ cup] **sour cream**

Grate the onion. Cut the slices of salami into thin strips.
Mix the cream cheese with the sour cream, add the onion and the salami strips, mix well and serve with potato crisps [chips.]

Pizza Toast

Preparation and cooking time:
20 minutes
SERVES 8

8 slices of white bread
1 oz. [2 tablespoons] **butter**
1 small onion, finely chopped
1 tablespoon olive oil
2 tablespoons tomato purée
8 large black olives
4 anchovy fillets, finely chopped
½ teaspoon basil, dried
4 oz. [1 cup] **grated Gruyère** [Swiss] **cheese**

Heat the grill [broiler].
Cut the crusts from the slices of bread and cut the slices in half. Fry in the butter until golden but not brown. Drain on absorbent kitchen paper.
Finely chop the onion and fry in the oil until soft, add the tomato purée and cook for another minute. Place in a small mixing bowl.
Stone the black olives and chop the flesh. Add them to the onion mixture.
Finely chop the anchovy fillets and mix with the rest.
Add the tomato and the basil and mix well.
Spread the mixture on the fried bread, sprinkle with the grated cheese and place under a hot grill [broiler] for 5-7 minutes.

Tuna Fish Pâté

Preparation and cooking time:
15 minutes
SERVES 8

8 oz. canned tuna fish
6 oz. [¾ cup] **butter**
2 tablespoons lemon juice
2 tablespoons olive oil
2 tablespoons brandy
1 garlic clove, crushed
1 tablespoon chopped parsley
1 medium-sized onion, peeled and grated
salt and pepper

Drain the tuna fish and melt the butter.
Mash the tuna fish with the lemon juice, olive oil and brandy. Add the melted butter, garlic, parsley, grated onion and seasoning. Beat until smooth, or put in an electric blender.
Adjust the seasoning and refrigerate until required.
Serve with hot toast.

Avocado and Cheese Dip

Preparation time:
15 minutes
MAKES about 1½ lb.

3 medium-sized avocado pears
3 tablespoons mayonnaise
4 drops tabasco
2 tablespoons lemon juice
2 tablespoons grated onion
1 garlic clove, crushed
2 oz. [½ cup] **strong cheese, grated**
4 fl. oz. double [½ cup heavy] **cream**
salt and pepper

Peel and stone the avocados. Using a wooden spoon push the avocado flesh through a strainer into a bowl, or use a food mill.
Mix in the mayonnaise, tabasco sauce, lemon juice, grated onion, crushed

garlic and grated cheese.
Beat the cream until stiff and fold into the avocado mixture.
Season with salt and pepper.
Cover the bowl and refrigerate until well chilled.
Serve with Julienne sticks of fresh raw vegetables, potato crisps [chips] or biscuits [crackers].

Salami on Black Bread

Preparation time:
15 minutes
SERVES 8

4 slices dark rye bread
1 oz. [2 tablespoons] **butter**
8 lettuce leaves
2 medium-sized onions
24 slices salami, thinly cut
8 parsley sprigs

Cut the slices of rye bread into halves and butter them. Place a lettuce leaf on top of each slice.
Thinly slice the onions and push into rings.
Fold the salami slices loosely in half and arrange 3 slices on each slice of bread.
Garnish with sprigs of parsley and the smallest of the onion rings.

Cheese Aigrettes

Preparation and cooking time:
35-45 minutes
SERVES 8

3 oz. [6 tablespoons] **butter**
8 fl. oz. [1 cup] **stock made up from ½ chicken stock cube**
5 oz. [1¼ cups] **flour, sifted**
4 eggs, beaten
2 oz. [½ cup] **Gruyère cheese, grated**
2 oz. [½ cup] **Parmesan cheese, grated**
a pinch of cayenne pepper
½ teaspoon dry mustard
salt and pepper
sufficient oil for deep frying

Heat oven to 300°F (Gas Mark 2, 150°C).
Place the butter and the stock in a saucepan and bring to the boil.
Remove the pan from the stove and tip all the flour in quickly. Beat well until the mixture is smooth and leaves the sides of the pan.
Beat in the eggs gradually. The grated cheese, cayenne pepper, dry mustard and a little salt and pepper and mix well.
Heat the oil in a heavy saucepan and drop in teaspoonfuls of the mixture. Fry for 7-10 minutes until golden brown.
Drain well on kitchen paper and keep warm in the oven until ready to serve.

Garlic Mayonnaise with Raw Vegetables

Preparation time:
30 minutes
SERVES 8

10 fl. oz. [1¼ cups] **aioli (see page 24)**
4 celery stalks
4 medium-sized carrots
24 small spring onions [scallions]

Make the aioli.
Scrape and cut the carrots in to ½-inch wide and 2-inches long sticks.
Wash and scrub the celery stalks and cut into similar sized pieces.
Trim and wash the spring onions [scallions].
Spoon the aioli into a tall stemmed glass, and surround with neat piles of the vegetable sticks and spring onions [scallions].

Cheese and Caraway Strips

  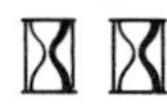

Preparation and cooking time:
50 minutes
MAKES about 18 strips

8 oz. frozen puff pastry, defrosted
1 egg, lightly beaten
4 oz. [1 cup] **strong cheese, grated or crumbled**
2 tablespoons caraway seeds

Roll out the pastry to a rectangle about 18-inches by 6-inches, and cut this in half to make two pieces, each about 18-inches by 3-inches.
Brush one of the halves with the beaten egg, and sprinkle this surface evenly with the cheese. Cover with the second half of the pastry, and press down firmly.
Cut the pastry sandwich into about 18 long strips, and place them on a lightly greased baking tray. Brush again with the egg, and sprinkle the caraway seeds evenly over the top.
Heat oven to 450°F (Gas Mark 8, 230°C).
Leave the strips in a cool place for about 15-20 minutes, and then bake for 8-10 minutes, until they have risen and are golden brown.
Serve hot.

Cucumber Cups with Crab Salad

Preparation time:
20 minutes
MAKES 8

1 large cucumber
2 eggs, hard-boiled
½ teaspoon celery salt
8 tablespoons mayonnaise (see page 62)
4 oz. canned crab meat, drained
To garnish:
fresh sprigs of dill weed or parsley

Slice the ends off the cucumber and discard. Cut the remainder into 8 equal pieces. Hollow out each piece so that it resembles an egg-cup.
Chop the eggs. Mix the mayonnaise with the celery salt and add the crab meat and chopped egg.
Carefully spoon the mixture into the cucumber cups, and garnish with sprigs of fresh dill weed or parsley.
Serve very cold.

right: Cheese Aigrettes
below: a country atmosphere may be created by such accessories as these, arranged on a scrubbed wooden surface.

PICNIC PARTY

Eating out of doors is an adventure which adults seem to enjoy almost as much as children. As the cities become more and more congested, so the need grows to get away, even if only for a few hours, into the peace and quiet of the countryside.

A picnic can range from fresh bread, cheese and a can of beer in the saddle bag of a bike, to a proper lunch at the races. But above all picnics should be fun. (All you need is the right weather!)

Organising the picnic

It is advisable to pick a spot which you know is suitable, and where picnicking is allowed. There is nothing worse than sitting down under a blue sky with all the food laid out, only to be moved on by an irate farmer or landowner. Setting off into the blue is exciting for children, but frustrating if you can't find the right place to stop.

Start early, and if you are meeting friends make sure they have an accurate map, with an obvious landmark like a church marked as a rendezvous. An amusing and inexpensive way of throwing a picnic party is to invite twenty or thirty people, asking each to bring their own food and wine. Everything is pooled on arrival, the organizer simply providing plates, cups, knives etc. Check that you have essential items like corkscrews and salt before you leave, and add some mosquito repellant, too.

Packing the food

Transporting the food need not involve buying an expensive wicker picnic basket, but it does require a selection of different shaped airtight containers in which to keep everything fresh and unsquashed. Wrap sandwiches, bread and rolls in a damp

left: A family picnic with a simple gingham cloth, plates and mugs—ideal for a country setting.
below: Fish Sandwich Cake

cloth or tinfoil; keep soup and coffee hot in wide mouthed vacuum flasks, and if possible take an insulated container or ice bags for keeping wine, pop and milk cold.

Making everyone comfortable
Make sure you have enough rugs and cushions for everyone to relax on. Three or four inflatable air mattresses are easy to transport and perfect for sitting on or against. Lay the food out on a large rug covered with a bright paper or linen tablecloth in a dry, sheltered spot. If you are lighting a fire, make sure it is sited well away from trees or dry grass, and in a down wind position from the picnic party.

Iced Carrot Soup

 ① 

Preparation and cooking time:
40 minutes
SERVES 8

1 lb. young carrots
4 stalks of celery
1 small onion
1 bayleaf
½ teaspoon salt
½ teaspoon white pepper
2 cloves
1½ pints [3¾ cups] **chicken stock made from stock cubes**
2 tablespoons chopped parsley
3 slices white bread
2 tablespoons olive oil
4 fl. oz. single [½ cup light] **cream**

Scrape and slice the carrots. Wash and slice the celery stalks. Slice the onion.
In a large saucepan combine the carrots, celery, onion, seasoning and chicken stock. Bring to the boil, then simmer over a moderate heat until the vegetables are quite soft.
Remove the pan from the stove and pour the contents through a strainer into a large bowl. Press the vegetables through the strainer with a wooden spoon, or use a food mill.
Stir in the chopped parsley and adjust the seasoning. Refrigerate until very cold; take on the picnic in a vacuum flask.
Cut the crusts from the slices of bread then dice the slices. Heat the oil in a frying pan and sauté the croûtons until golden brown. Take out, drain on kitchen paper, when cool pack in an airtight container. Pack the cream separately.
Before serving the soup stir in the cream and sprinkle with the croûtons.

Fish Sandwich Cake

 ① ① ①

Preparation time:
1 hour
SERVES 8

4 oz. cooked, peeled prawns or shrimps
8 oz. [1 cup] **butter, at room temperature**
salt and pepper
3½ oz. canned sardines
1 tablespoon chopped parsley
juice of 1 lemon
6 oz. canned Danish caviare [lumpfish roe]
3½ oz. canned salmon
1 tablespoon tomato purée
2 small sweet pickled gherkins, finely chopped
1 lb. square sandwich loaf (preferably 1 day old)
8 fl. oz. [1 cup] **thick mayonnaise (see page 62)**
4 slices smoked salmon
To garnish:
1 lemon, sliced
1 lettuce

First make the fillings.
Prawn or shrimp filling: mash the prawns or shrimps with 2 ounces [4 tablespoons] of the butter. Season with salt and freshly ground pepper. Set aside.
Sardine filling: drain the sardines and mash the fish with 2 ounces [4 tablespoons] of the butter, the chopped parsley and 1 teaspoon of lemon juice. Set aside.
Danish caviare [lumpfish roe] filling: carefully mix half the caviare [lumpfish roe] with 2 ounces of [4 tablespoons] the butter. Set aside.
Salmon filling: drain the salmon and mash the meat with the rest of the butter, the tomato purée and the chopped gherkins. Set aside.
Remove the crusts from the loaf and slice it in to 5 lengthwise.
Spread each slice with one of the fillings. Re-form the original loaf shape by placing the slices on top of each other, adding the plain bread slice last.
Wrap in aluminium foil and refrigerate for about 2 hours.
Cut the smoked salmon into thin strips. Place the gâteau in a suitable container.
At the picnic site coat the cake with the mayonnaise. Cover the sides with the rest of the caviare [lumpfish roe] and arrange the slices of smoked salmon on top.
Garnish with twists of lemons and lettuce leaves.

Chicken with Juniper Berries

① ① 

Preparation and cooking time:
1¼ hours
SERVES 8

4 oz. [½ cup] **butter**
2 tablespoons olive oil
2 large onions, finely chopped
4 tablespoons chopped parsley
10 juniper berries, lightly crushed
2 x 3 lb. roasting chickens
16 fl. oz. [2 cups] **dry white wine**
6 tablespoons gin
2 teaspoons salt
freshly ground pepper
16 fl. oz. double [2 cups heavy] **cream**

Heat the butter and the oil in a saucepan large enough to hold the 2 chickens.
Add the chopped onions, chopped parsley and the crushed juniper berries and sauté until the onions are slightly brown.
Add the chickens and fry, turning them until they are evenly browned.
Add the wine, gin, salt and freshly ground pepper.
Cover and simmer for 30 minutes.
Remove from the heat and leave the chickens in the stock until they are cold. Take them out, remove the skin and pull the meat off the bones. Place in a suitable container.
Pour the stock through a strainer, and with a wooden spoon, push as much of the cooked onions through as possible. Leave to cool.
Whip the cream until stiff and, little by little, beat in as much stock as is necessary to make a consistency like a thinnish mayonnaise. Spoon this over the chicken meat. Serve with a rice salad and a cucumber salad.

Mayonnaise Barbecue Sauce

Preparation and cooking time:
15 minutes
MAKES about 15 fl. oz. [2 cups]

10 fl. oz. [$1\frac{1}{4}$ cup] **mayonnaise** (see page 62)
6 fl. oz. double [$\frac{3}{4}$ cup heavy] **cream**
3 tablespoons tomato purée
2 teaspoons Worcestershire sauce
1 teaspoon soy sauce
$\frac{1}{2}$ teaspoon salt
freshly ground black pepper

Mix the mayonnaise with all the other ingredients. Do not heat.

Barbecue sauce

Preparation and cooking time:
30 minutes
MAKES 15 fl. oz. [about 2 cups]

3 tablespoons cider vinegar
5 fl. oz. [$\frac{5}{8}$ cup] **water**
3 tablespoons sugar
2 tablespoons English mustard
2 garlic cloves, crushed
freshly ground black pepper
1 teaspoon salt
1 medium-sized onion, finely chopped
5 fl. oz. [$\frac{5}{8}$ cup] **tomato ketchup**
grated zest of 1 lemon
juice of 1 lemon
1 tablespoon Worcestershire sauce
2 oz. [4 tablespoons] **butter**

In a saucepan mix together all the ingredients and heat until just below boiling point. Do not boil. Simmer for 20 minutes.

BARBECUE PARTY

opposite: Chicken with Orange and Figs

There is no doubt that food eaten and cooked out of doors acquires a special quality all of its own. Up to a point this may be due to appetites which are sharpened by the fresh air, but the flavour of meat and fish, if correctly prepared, is definitely enhanced by the slow gentle heat of a wood or charcoal fire.
You can spend as little or as much as you like on equipment (two metal boot scrapers or a length of chicken wire laid over the fire will make an adequate grill). There are tiny portable barbecues available which can be used on a balcony, or you can buy one of the excellent mobile affairs which come complete with automatic spit roasts and drip trays.

Fuel
Loose charcoal or briquettes are the ideal fuel since they burn slowly and produce an even heat. Dry, well seasoned wood can be used, but maintaining a steady heat can be tricky. Start the fire with fire lighters or a small quantity of methylated spirits—*never* petrol [gasoline].

The right heat
Light the fire about three quarters of an hour before you intend to eat. The right moment to start cooking is when the charcoal has acquired a dull overall glow without flames or sparks.

Let your guests play cavemen
Allow those who want to a chance to play cavemen round the fire with a big mound of sausages for children, kebabs, chicken pieces, spareribs or fresh sardines for adults. Simply brush the meat beforehand with olive oil, and season lightly with salt and freshly ground black pepper.

Gammon and Pineapple Kebabs

 ① ① 

Preparation and cooking time:
40 minutes
SERVES 8

1½ lb. gammon [ham] **slices, ½-inch thick**
2 oz. [4 tablespoons] **butter**
1 lb. canned pineapple cubes
32 large bayleaves

Cut the rind from the gammon [ham] and remove any surplus fat. Cut into ½-inch cubes.
Melt the butter in a frying-pan and sauté the gammon [ham] cubes for 5 minutes.
Drain the pineapple cubes.
Arrange the gammon and pineapple cubes with the bayleaves on 8 skewers and barbecue for 20-30 minutes, depending on how hot the charcoal is.
Turn and baste frequently.

Pork Steaks
with gherkins and mushroom sauce

 ① ① 

Preparation and cooking time:
30 minutes
SERVES 8

4 pork fillets
4 large sweet pickled gherkins
salt and pepper
For the mushroom sauce:
8 oz. button mushrooms
1 oz. [2 tablespoons] **butter**
4 fl. oz. [½ cup] **stock**
10 fl. oz. double [1¼ cups heavy] **cream**
1 tablespoon soy sauce
½ teaspoon salt
2 tablespoons dry sherry

Cut the pork fillets in half, removing sinews and surplus fat. Beat the meat flat with a meat-hammer.
Slice the gherkins into 4 slices, lengthwise. Place the meat on the hot barbecue and cook for 5-7 minutes on each side. Cook the gherkins for 3-4 minutes on each side (place them on foil on the barbecue).
Make the mushroom sauce by wiping clean the mushrooms and slicing them thinly.
Melt the butter in a saucepan and sauté the mushrooms for a few minutes. Add all the remaining ingredients and cook for 3-4 minutes.
Place the gherkins on top of the pork fillets and pour the mushroom sauce over.

Note: The mushroom sauce may be prepared in advance, and reheated at the barbecue site.

Roasted Apples on Skewers

 ① 

Preparation and cooking time:
20 minutes
SERVES 8

8 dessert apples
8 skewers
For the sauce:
4 tablespoons butter
4 tablespoons gin
6 tablespoons grapefruit juice
3 tablespoons sugar

Secure the apples on the skewers and cook over the fire. It is much easier if each person cooks his own apple.
Make the sauce by melting the butter in a small pan and adding the other ingredients.
Keep warm and dip the apples in the sauce before eating.

Chicken with Orange and Figs

 ① 

Preparation and cooking time:
40 minutes
SERVES 8

16 chicken portions
2 oz. [4 tablespoons] **butter**
3 large oranges
16 fresh or dried figs

Melt the butter in a large frying-pan and sauté the chicken portions for 5-6 minutes. This cuts down the barbecue time.
Cut each orange into 6 segments.
Arrange on 8 skewers the chicken pieces, orange segments and the figs.
Baste frequently with the barbecue sauce and grill for 30 minutes or until the chicken is cooked.

ZODIAC PARTYSCOPE

An unusual and colourful way of celebrating an adult or teenage birthday is to give a Zodiac Party, where the decorative effects are based on the various signs. If the celebration is a small dinner party, for example, each guest could be given their own Zodiac place mat, and a horoscope rolled up inside their napkin. Bright, gypsy style colours could be used to highlight each individual setting, perhaps set against a dramatic black and white astrological motif tablecloth—you could design this yourself on thick paper. The Zodiac theme can also be used as the basis of a fancy dress party where each person is asked to come dressed to represent their own particular sign. Alternatively small informal parties can be organised where all the guests are born under the same sign.

The style and mood of any party is dictated to a great extent by the personality of the host. The extrovert Scorpio entertainer for instance will fill his or her home with crowds of people and create a colourful, vibrant atmosphere. The less flamboyant Cancer host will prefer to create a more relaxed setting, where a handful of really close friends may enjoy each other's company and have time to appreciate some rather special dish or wine. Everyone has different ideas about what constitutes a good party, as the following Partyscope shows.

Aries *March 21st — April 20th*
Aries people are fiery, generous and passionate. They like to give and go to no-expense-spared parties, often on the spur of the moment with lots of new faces and plenty of noise. They are imaginative entertainers, but worry little about cost.

Taurus *April 21st — May 21st*
Taurians like a quiet well-ordered home life in which they can entertain close friends. They like to eat and drink well, but never frivolously. They enjoy spicy food and good conversation which they will often keep going until the early hours.

Gemini *May 22nd — June 22nd*
The Geminian is full of nervous energy. He or she will prefer to go to rather than to give a party, but when Geminis do entertain they do so with a purpose and with great style. They have a craving for novelty and love surrounding themselves with new acquaintances.

Cancer *June 23rd — July 23rd*
The Cancer entertainer likes to feel secure. He or she will prefer to give small intimate parties for people who share similar tastes. Cancer people thrive on the praise and affection of others, so care is usually taken to prepare special dishes for special guests and to create a romantic setting.

Leo *July 24th — August 23rd*

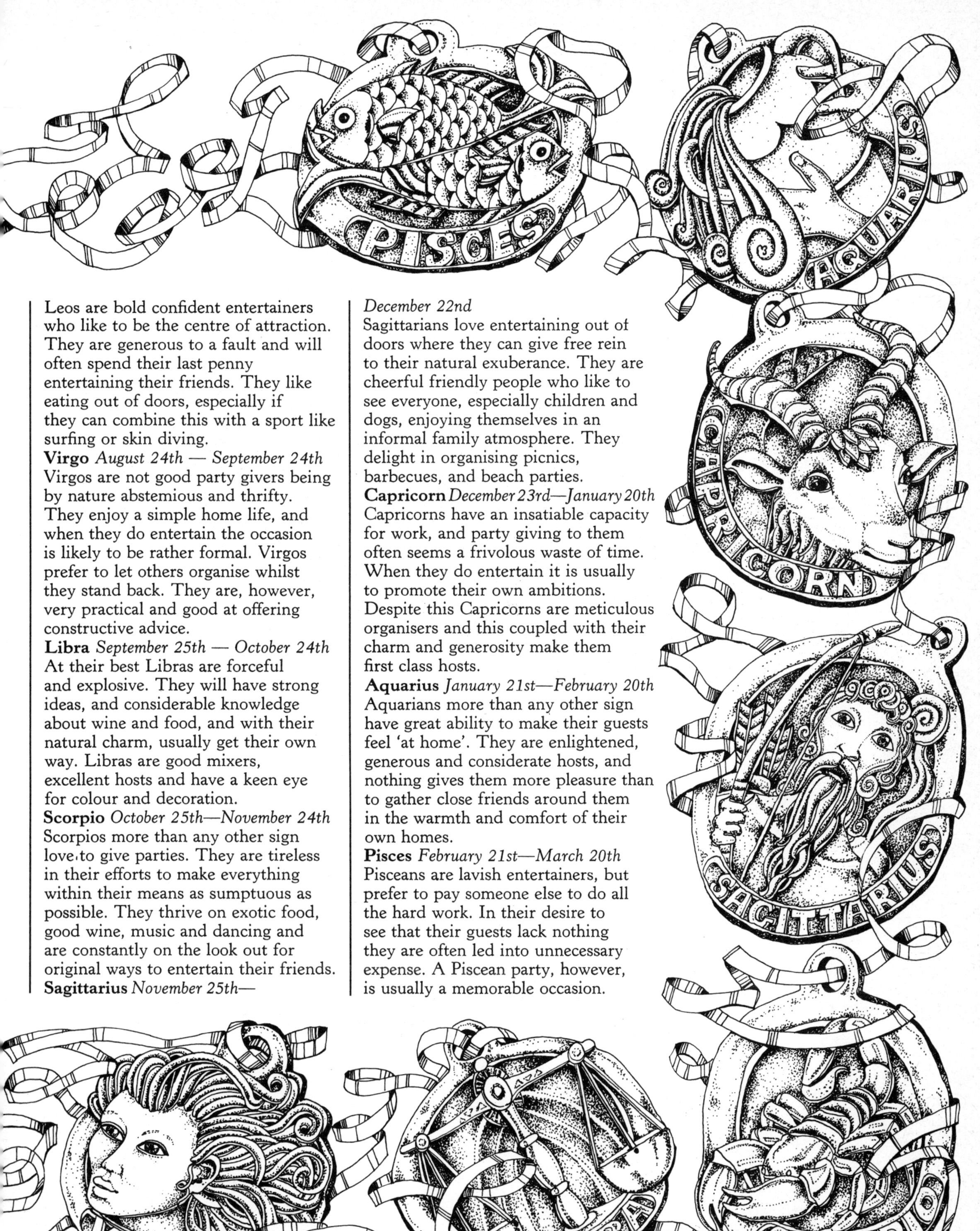

Leos are bold confident entertainers who like to be the centre of attraction. They are generous to a fault and will often spend their last penny entertaining their friends. They like eating out of doors, especially if they can combine this with a sport like surfing or skin diving.

Virgo *August 24th — September 24th*
Virgos are not good party givers being by nature abstemious and thrifty. They enjoy a simple home life, and when they do entertain the occasion is likely to be rather formal. Virgos prefer to let others organise whilst they stand back. They are, however, very practical and good at offering constructive advice.

Libra *September 25th — October 24th*
At their best Libras are forceful and explosive. They will have strong ideas, and considerable knowledge about wine and food, and with their natural charm, usually get their own way. Libras are good mixers, excellent hosts and have a keen eye for colour and decoration.

Scorpio *October 25th—November 24th*
Scorpios more than any other sign love to give parties. They are tireless in their efforts to make everything within their means as sumptuous as possible. They thrive on exotic food, good wine, music and dancing and are constantly on the look out for original ways to entertain their friends.

Sagittarius *November 25th—December 22nd*
Sagittarians love entertaining out of doors where they can give free rein to their natural exuberance. They are cheerful friendly people who like to see everyone, especially children and dogs, enjoying themselves in an informal family atmosphere. They delight in organising picnics, barbecues, and beach parties.

Capricorn *December 23rd—January 20th*
Capricorns have an insatiable capacity for work, and party giving to them often seems a frivolous waste of time. When they do entertain it is usually to promote their own ambitions. Despite this Capricorns are meticulous organisers and this coupled with their charm and generosity make them first class hosts.

Aquarius *January 21st—February 20th*
Aquarians more than any other sign have great ability to make their guests feel 'at home'. They are enlightened, generous and considerate hosts, and nothing gives them more pleasure than to gather close friends around them in the warmth and comfort of their own homes.

Pisces *February 21st—March 20th*
Pisceans are lavish entertainers, but prefer to pay someone else to do all the hard work. In their desire to see that their guests lack nothing they are often led into unnecessary expense. A Piscean party, however, is usually a memorable occasion.

1966
Charles
FINEST EXTRA

SPECIAL OCCASIONS

opposite: Anniversary party: Pheasant Casserole, and Sole with Peppers and Shrimps

There are a number of days in the year which call for a special kind of party, or at any rate make an ideal excuse for having a party. Some of them are much more widely celebrated than others, but they all have the advantage of having a specific theme or traditional background to which may be added your own personal touches.

November 5th
Guy Fawkes' Night is essentially an evening for children, but it offers a good opportunity for several families to get together for a party. To avoid everyone trailing into the house with muddy boots, set up a tressle table near the bonfire to serve food and drink. The heat will keep everyone warm and provide light to see by. As soon as the fireworks are over serve a Hot Toddy (see page 14) for the adults, and hot chocolate or soup for children. As small hands may be cold keep everything the children eat easy to handle, baby hot dogs, using half sausages in bridge rolls are ideal, followed by home made toffee apples. For adults, try a selection of *quiches* or hot *bouchées* with a variety of fillings.

Halloween
Halloween takes place on the night of October 31st. It is an evening when the werewolf stalks, and things are meant to go bump in the night. For young children and teenagers it is a wonderful chance to use all their powers of imagination to create a spooky atmosphere with cut out witches, weird lighting effects and strange masks. Adults may be asked to come dressed as witches and demons for a wine and cheese party or buffet supper, with the host providing the appropriate setting with a predominantly black theme.

New Year's Eve
New Year's Eve parties tend to be boisterous affairs which require careful planning and control over numbers to avoid disaster. It is a good idea to start the party late, say 10 pm, with a substantial buffet available as soon as everyone arrives. Extra people often seem to turn up on New Year's Eve, so make your initial guest list smaller than you would normally. Hot and cold wine punches are less inflammatory than straight spirits, but some people make it traditional to welcome the new year in with champagne. It is a practical idea to have a cup of hot soup or coffee available for guests, as they leave.

Christmas Eve
The evening of December 24th is probably the most enjoyable part of Christmas. It is a time for families and close friends to relax over present wrapping and tree decorating and think what Christmas is all about. In view of the rigours of the following day an early, informal supper round the fire is ideal, or a simple light buffet with home made pâtés, a selection of salads, and—to get in the mood—mince pies with brandy butter. A hot, spicy rum punch or egg nog is a nice way of welcoming carol singers or for that matter anyone who calls unexpectedly.

Shrove Tuesday
Shrove Tuesday, the day before the the beginning of Lent in the Christian calendar, offers an ideal opportunity to give an informal party where the food is based on a whole range of delicious sweet or savoury pancakes. Try Russian blinis—served with melted butter and sour cream—or for special occasions caviar or smoked salmon. *Crêpes aux fruits de mer*—pancakes stuffed with a creamy shellfish mixture—would make another good choice. Or try American breakfast pancakes served with grilled [broiled] sausages, crisp bacon and maple syrup—or even magnificent *crêpes Suzette* flaming in brandy and Cointreau. Keep numbers small, so that each guest gets freshly made pancakes.

St. Valentine's Day
Anyone giving a St. Valentine's Day party should avoid the temptation of overdoing the hearts and flowers, especially where teenagers are concerned. A fancy dress party where everyone is asked to dress as a famous lover could produce some amusing results, or one based on the notorious St. Valentine's Day massacre of the 1920s, held in a garage perhaps with a honky tonk piano. For a touch of romance guests can be asked to bring a partner of their own choice.

Other occasions
Apart from the well known days in the year already mentioned, there are a number of other days and occasions which may be used as an excuse for getting one's friends together to have a party.
Older people always say they like to forget their birthdays, but it is surprising how delighted most of them are when somebody goes to the trouble of organising a small celebration on their behalf.
Mother's and Father's Day offer an opportunity for small informal family gatherings; St. Patrick's Night could be used for an Irish style party. An excellent present for anyone getting engaged, moving house or about to have a baby is to arrange a 'shower party' where guests bring a small present to celebrate the event.

AFTER~THEATRE PARTY

left: Chilled Spinach Soup
below: Turkey Pie, and Macaroon Cream with Grapes

Taking a party of friends to the theatre or cinema, or to any other evening event, can be happily rounded-off by a home cooked meal. Preparing supper at home naturally requires time and effort, but in the long run is more rewarding, and less expensive, than dining out.
The after-theatre supper party demands a choice of food that requires the minimum amount of last-minute effort. Everything should be prepared beforehand, so that as the host you may give all your attention to mixing drinks and making the guests comfortable. Since the chances are that no one will have eaten since lunch, speed is essential—and guests should not have to wait longer for their food than it takes to down one stiff drink. Make sure everyone has something to nibble with the drink, and in winter see that the rooms are warm and cosy. Drawing curtains, stacking the fire, laying out drinks and having candles ready to light on the table are jobs that can be done before leaving, so that it only takes a few minutes for the host to make everything look bright and cheerful for the returning party. If possible it is preferable to meet guests at the entertainment, rather than giving everyone drinks at home beforehand, as this avoids returning to dirty glasses and ashtrays!
As the meal will be late, it is advisable, purely for digestive reasons, to keep the menu light and simple. One hot course is quite sufficient, and should be balanced by relatively light cold dishes.

Chilled Spinach Soup

①

Preparation and cooking time:
40 minutes
SERVES 8

1 lb. fresh spinach
1 medium-sized onion, chopped
1 oz. [2 tablespoons] **butter**
1 oz. [¼ cup] **flour**
2 pints [5 cups] **milk**
salt and pepper
2 egg yolks
4 fl. oz. double [½ cup heavy] **cream**
To garnish:
2 hard boiled eggs, finely chopped

Wash and drain the spinach. Discard the stalks and chop coarsely.
Melt the butter in a large saucepan and fry the onion until soft but not brown. Add the spinach and stew gently for 5 to 6 minutes. Draw aside and mix in the flour.
Bring the milk to the boil and pour over the spinach. Add salt and pepper and return the pan to the stove. Bring to the boil and simmer for 15 to 20 minutes.
Make a liaison by mixing the egg yolks and cream. Blend or sieve the soup.
Return the soup to the saucepan, mix with the liaison and bring to the boil. Correct the seasoning. Pour into a bowl and chill.
Serve garnished with the chopped hard-boiled egg.

Turkey Pie

 ① ① 

Preparation and cooking time:
2 hours
SERVES 8

4 large carrots
16 button mushrooms
4 leeks
2 onions
1½ lb. turkey meat
3 oz. [6 tablespoons] **butter**
1½ pints [3¾ cups] **chicken stock, made from 1 stock cube**
10 juniper berries
salt and pepper
12 oz. puff pastry (**see page 61**)
1 egg, beaten

Heat oven to 400°F (Gas Mark 6, 200°C). Scrape and slice the carrots, wipe the mushrooms. Trim the leeks, wash them well, then slice. Slice the onions. Cut the turkey meat into cubes.
Melt 2 ounces [4 tablespoons] of the butter in a large saucepan and sauté the chopped vegetables until they are lightly browned. Add the stock and cook for 5 minutes. Strain the stock into a pitcher and put the vegetables and the cubes of turkey in a deep 2-pint pie dish.
Crush the juniper berries and add to the pie dish. Season well with salt and pepper.
Melt the rest of the butter in a saucepan. Remove the pan from the heat and, with a wooden spoon, stir in the flour to make a smooth paste. Gradually stir in the stock, stirring constantly. Return the pan to the heat and cook for a further few minutes until the sauce has thickened slightly. Correct the seasoning and pour it over the turkey and vegetables.
Roll out the pastry on a floured table or board to 1-inch larger than the top of the pie dish. With a knife cut a ½-inch strip from the pastry. Moisten the rim of the pie dish with water and press the pastry strip on top of the rim. With a pastry brush, dipped in water, lightly moisten the strip. Using a rolling pin lift the dough on to the dish.
Trim the dough and, with a knife, crimp the edges to seal them to the strip already on the dish.
Coat the surface of the pie with egg.
Use the trimmings to make decorations on top of the pie. Make a slit in the top.
Place in the oven and bake for 1 hour or until the top is golden brown.

Note: Prepare the pie earlier in the day, and re-heat for 20-30 minutes before serving (use the same setting as for the original cooking).

Macaroon Cream with Grapes

① ① 

Preparation and cooking time:
30 minutes
SERVES 8

1 lb. grapes
½ oz. gelatine
4 tablespoons water
16 macaroons
4 fl. oz. [½ cup] **medium-dry sherry**
10 fl. oz. double [1¼ cups heavy] **cream**
4 egg whites
4 tablespoons vanilla sugar
2 tablespoons grated plain [semi-sweet] **chocolate**

Peel and halve the grapes. Remove the pips.
Soak the gelatine in the water for 5 minutes before dissolving over a gentle heat. Set aside to cool.
Use 8 individual dessert glasses. Place 2 macaroons in each and sprinkle with the sherry.
Whip the cream until it is very stiff.
Whisk the egg whites until stiff, beat in the vanilla sugar and fold in the cream.
When the gelatine is cool mix it into the egg-white mixture. Add the peeled grapes, stir gently and spoon this on top of the macaroons.
Leave in the refrigerator until set.
Decorate with the grated chocolate.

ANNIVERSARY PARTY

An anniversary party is given to mark an important occasion in somebody's life. Anniversaries are usually informal gatherings of close friends and relatives, and it is up to the person organising the party to create a warm and intimate atmosphere in which reminiscences can flourish, and to provide food and wine to match the event.

A dinner party of six to ten people is an ideal way of celebrating any anniversary. Start the evening with something bubbly like champagne, a champagne-based cocktail, or (if your pocket permits) it would be an

below: Celeriac with Poached Egg and Smoked Salmon

impressive touch to buy a magnum, and to ask all the guests to sign the label before dinner.
Choose a menu which has at least one rather special luxury item on it, say turtle soup or smoked salmon to start, or duck or pheasant as a main course.
It is a delightful idea to order a special cake or *bombe surprise* which can be decorated with a light hearted message and arrayed with candles.
If you're lashing out, ask your wine merchant to find one or two rather special bottles of wine for you, say a Burgundy whose vintage date has a special significance for the guest of honour, or an old port or brandy with which to end dinner.
Finally, if everyone you would like to ask can't be fitted in round the table, ask them to come after dinner for coffee, liqueurs and a piece of that special cake.

Celeriac

with poached egg and smoked salmon

 ① ① ① ⧗ ⧗

Preparation and cooking time:
1 hour 15 minutes
SERVES 8

2 large celeriac roots
8 eggs
8 slices smoked salmon
8 tablespoons mayonnaise (**see page 62**)
2 lemons, thinly sliced
To garnish:
watercress

Cut away the leaves and the root fibres of the celeriac. Boil in salted water for 40-50 minutes, until cooked. Drain, peel and set aside to cool. Cut 4 slices from the centre of each celeriac, each about ½-inch thick. Place each on a serving dish.
Poach the eggs and set aside to cool.
Place a poached egg on top of each slice of celeriac. Arrange the smoked salmon neatly on the side of the plate. Add a spoonful of mayonnaise to the plate. Place a twisted slice of lemon on top of each portion.
Serve garnished with watercress.

Note: Any celeriac left over may be added to stock.

Sole with Peppers and Shrimps

☆ ☆ ① ① ① ⧗

Preparation and cooking time:
30 minutes
SERVES 8

8 fillets of sole
salt and pepper
10 fl. oz. [1¼ cups] **white wine**
8 fl. oz. [1 cup] **water**
2 green peppers
4 oz. [1 cup] **cooked, peeled, fresh prawns or shrimps**
3 oz. [6 tablespoons] **butter**
2 oz. [½ cup] **flour**
2½ fl. oz. single [¼ cup light] **cream**
To garnish:
3 tablespoons chopped parsley

Heat oven to 375°F (Gas Mark 5, 190°C).
Season the fillets of sole with salt and pepper and place in a shallow ovenproof dish. Pour the wine and the water over the fillets and cover the dish with aluminium foil. Poach in the oven for 10-15 minutes.
Meanwhile wash the peppers and remove the core and seeds. Cut the flesh into strips and sauté in 1 ounce [2 tablespoons] of the butter until soft. Put aside.
Strain off the poaching liquid, reserve, and keep the fish fillets hot in the covered dish.
Melt the rest of the butter in a saucepan. Remove the pan from the heat and, with a wooden spoon, stir in the flour to make a smooth paste. Gradually add the reserved liquid, stirring constantly. Return the pan to the heat and cook, stirring constantly, for 2-3 minutes or until the sauce is thick and smooth.
Add the prawns or shrimps, green peppers and cream to the pan, stir and pour the sauce over the fillets of sole.
Serve sprinkled with the parsley.

Pheasant Casserole

☆ ☆ ① ① ① ⧗ ⧗ ⧗

Preparation and cooking time:
2½ hours
SERVES 8

3 young, oven-ready pheasants
4 oz. [½ cup] **butter**
4 slices bacon
20 small onions or shallots
20 button mushrooms
1 lb. canned water-chestnuts
16 fl. oz. [2 cups] **red wine**
2 bayleaves
2 sprigs of fresh thyme
salt and pepper
8 fl. oz. single [1 cup light] **cream**
4 tablespoons brandy

Heat oven to 325°F (Gas Mark 3, 170°C).
Melt the butter in a large frying pan and sauté the birds until well browned on all sides. Remove from the pan and set aside.
Cut the rinds off the bacon and dice the meat.
Skin the onions, wipe clean the mushrooms and cut off the stalks.
Drain the water-chestnuts and slice thinly.
Put the bacon into the frying pan and sauté in the remaining butter until crisp, then transfer to a large casserole.
Fry the onions gently for a few minutes, then add the mushrooms and fry for another 3-4 minutes. Put them in the casserole with the bacon. Add the pheasants, water-chestnuts, wine and bayleaves, and cook in the oven for 1 hour.
Remove the casserole from the oven, take out the bayleaves, turn over the birds and stir in the cream.
Ignite the brandy and add to the casserole.
Cover and return to the oven for a further ½-hour.
When the birds are cooked remove all the food, strain the juice into a jug, and clean out the casserole.
Replace the bacon, onions, mushrooms and water-chestnuts in the casserole.
Carve the birds, add them to the casserole, and keep hot.
Adjust the seasoning in the gravy and pour this over the birds.
Serve with boiled new potatoes and a watercress and orange salad.

Note

End the meal with a good selection of cheeses, and fresh fruit. Try apples with Cheddar, blue cheeses with pears, and a creamy cheese with fresh figs, if these are available.

Today's teenager frequently seems to be a rather sophisticated character, but it is also true that many are often shy, and feel unsure of themselves in company. Because of this it is an excellent idea to create a total atmosphere for a teenage party—it gives everyone something to talk about when they first arrive, puts them in the right mood, and makes it easy to relax and have fun.
An attic or garage is an ideal choice for the setting, and with inexpensive 'props' of your teenager's choice it's comparatively easy to assemble the scene.
Make sure that the lighting is warm and sympathetic, and that there is somewhere to dance. In summer a barbecue in the garden, with one room in the house set aside for music, is probably the perfect combination.
Teenagers like to be left on their own, so once the parents see that everything is under way, it is probably better to retire—making sure everyone knows when the party is due to end.

What to drink
What you offer your teenage guests to drink depends on their degree of sophistication. Most sixteen year olds like wine, but it is probably advisable to make it into a punch by the addition of fruit, ice and soda water. Serve lager, cider, coke, fresh fruit juice, or if it is a special occasion maybe one glass of champagne each to get things going.

What to eat
Keep food simple, but present it in an adult manner, and in keeping with the atmosphere. The food should be easy to eat—things like cold turkey or chicken salad with rice, or a whole baked ham, followed by a rich creamy pudding or home made ice cream, are ideal.

Pineapple Plaice with Curry Mayonnaise

 ① ① 

Preparation and cooking time:
45 minutes
SERVES 8

8 fillets of plaice [flounder]**, skinned**
salt and pepper
1 glass white wine
10 fl. oz. [1¼ cups] **water**
5 whole peppercorns
1 bayleaf
1 large pineapple
10 fl. oz. [1¼ cups] **curry mayonnaise (see page 62)**
To garnish:
2 lettuces
tomato slices and parsley sprigs

Heat oven to 375°F (Gas Mark 5, 190°C).
Season the plaice [flounder] with salt and pepper, roll each fillet up neatly and place them all in an ovenproof dish. Pour over the wine and water and add the peppercorns and bayleaf to the liquid.
Cover the dish with aluminium foil, place in the oven. Poach for 10-15 minutes. Remove the dish, and strain away the juice and set the plaice fillets aside. Allow to cool.
Cut the pineapple into 8 thick slices.
Wash the lettuce, discarding the outer leaves, and slice the tomatoes.
Arrange the pineapple slices on top of the lettuce leaves in a serving dish, or in 8 individual dishes. Put a rolled plaice [flounder] fillet on top of each and coat with the curry mayonnaise.
Garnish with tomato slices and sprigs of parsley.

Hamburgers

Preparation and cooking time:
35 minutes
SERVES 8

3 lbs. lean beef
1 large onion, grated
freshly ground black pepper
1 teaspoon salt
1 egg, beaten
8 soft rolls or sesame seed buns
To garnish:
3 onions, thinly sliced
a selection of ketchups or relishes

Heat the grill [broiler] on a high setting.
Mince [grind] the meat very finely and mix well with the grated onion, plenty of freshly ground black pepper, salt and the beaten egg.
Shape into 8 thick flat cakes and place under the hot grill [broiler], turning once, for 5-7 minutes, according to taste.
Serve immediately in plain soft rolls or in toasted sesame seeds buns with raw onions, mustard and tomato ketchup or with Yankee Tomato Relish.

Yankee Tomato Relish

☆ ① 

Preparation time:
15 minutes, plus 12 hours refrigeration
MAKES enough for 8 hamburgers

4 large tomatoes, skinned and chopped
1 green pepper, cored seeded and chopped
4 celery stalks, finely sliced
1 medium-sized onion, finely chopped
2 small pickled gherkins, chopped
3 tablespoons sugar
1 tablespoon English mustard
4 fl. oz. [½ cup] **wine veinegar**

Mix all the ingredients together well. Refrigerate for at least 12 hours before using.

Mocha Cup

 ① ① 

Preparation and cooking time:
30 minutes
SERVES 8-10

½ oz. gelatine
4 fl. oz. [½ cup] **strong black coffee**
4 eggs
4 oz. [½ cup] **sugar**
1 pint double [2½ cups heavy] **cream**
2 tablespoons Tia Maria or other flavoured liqueur
4 oz. dark [semi-sweet] **chocolate, grated**
2 oz. [½ cup] **chopped walnuts**

Soak the gelatine in the coffee for 5 minutes before dissolving over low heat. Set aside to cool slightly.
Separate the eggs. Cream the yolks with the sugar until very light and fluffy.
Whisk the cream until stiff and reserve half for decoration.
Whisk the egg whites until very stiff.
Mix the cool coffee and gelatine with the egg yolk and sugar mixture. Stir in the Tia Maria, grated chocolate and chopped walnuts. When the mixture begins to set fold in half of the whipped cream and then the stiff egg whites.
Pour into tall glasses and, when set, decorate with rosettes of whipped cream.

TEENAGE PARTY

right: Pineapple Plaice with Curry Mayonnaise
below right: Hamburgers in preparation
below: Decorations may be co-ordinated to produce a theme for the party room—here, an Eastern atmosphere creates instant young appeal.

INSTANT PARTY

left: Gingernut Cream
below: Ham-Wrapped Bananas

Anyone can be faced with having to give an instant party. A husband returns from the office with two extra for dinner, a party of lively friends drop in unannounced after a film, or maybe your boy friend decides at the last moment that he would rather eat at home than in a restaurant. What do you do? Like the boyscouts, the answer is—be prepared.
Unless you are lucky enough to live near a late night delicatessen the chances are that you will have to rely on a well-stocked store cupboard. Canned soups can be brought to life by the addition of sherry, cream and a knob of butter and served with crisp fried croûtons. Tuna fish blended with oil, lemon juice and black pepper makes a tasty pâté.
A stale loaf is not the end of the world. Break it up and toast it lightly in the oven and it will yield delicious crunchy chunks. Tinned salmon, although not as good as smoked haddock, will make a perfectly good kedgeree. Omelettes can be filled with practically anything from tinned tomatoes to onion and potato, and can be made to look and taste more professional by whipping the whites separately from the yolks. Sardines on toast, or Welsh rarebit made with lots of mustard and Worcestershire sauce are two savouries which are quick and easy to prepare from limited resources. And of course pasta, perhaps the most obvious of all standbys, can be used in lots of ways with canned sauces and meat dishes.
Make the table look attractive with crisp napkins and cloth, candles, and a decanter of wine.
After dinner Irish coffee makes an excellent alternative to liqueurs if th drink cupboard is running low.

Ham-Wrapped Bananas

Preparation and cooking time:
30 minutes
SERVES 8

4 oz. strong cheese
8 slices cooked ham
8 bananas
1½ oz. [3 tablespoons] **butter**
2 tablespoons flour
12 fl. oz. [1½ cups] **milk or stock**
1 teaspoon made English mustard
salt and pepper

Heat the grill [broiler].
Grate the cheese and cut away any fat from the ham.
Peel the bananas. Wrap them in slices of ham and place them in a lightly buttered heatproof dish.
Make a white sauce with the butter, flour and milk or stock. Add the mustard and half the grated cheese. Season with salt and pepper.
Pour the sauce over the ham and sprinkle with the rest of the cheese.
Place under the hot grill [broiler] and cook for 8-10 minutes or until the cheese is brown. Serve hot.

Variations:
Instead of bananas use canned asparagus or canned celery hearts.

Tunafish Vol-au-Vents

Preparation and cooking time:
30 minutes
SERVES 8

16 frozen vol-au-vent cases, defrosted
1 egg, beaten
14 oz. canned tuna fish
1 pint [2½ cups] **chicken stock, made from a chicken stock cube**
1 large onion
2 oz. [4 tablespoons] **butter**
¾ oz. [3 tablespoons] **flour**
½ teaspoon dried tarragon
1 tablespoon capers
salt and pepper

Heat oven to 400°F (Gas Mark 6, 200°C).
Place the vol-au-vent cases on a lightly greased baking sheet.
Brush the tops with egg and bake in the oven for 15-20 minutes.
While the cases are cooking drain the tuna fish, make the stock with the chicken stock cube and chop the onion.
Melt half the butter in a frying pan and fry the onion until soft and translucent but not brown. Put aside.
Melt the rest of the butter in a saucepan over moderate heat. Remove the pan from the stove and, with a wooden spoon, stir in the flour to make a smooth paste. Gradually add the stock, stirring constantly.
Return the saucepan to the heat and cook for 2-3 minutes, stirring well, until the sauce is thick and smooth. Add the tarragon, capers, onion and the tuna fish, breaking up the meat a little.
Season with salt and pepper and keep warm. When the vol-au-vent cases are cooked, take them out of the oven. Remove the lids and any soft dough in the centre.
Fill them with the tuna fish sauce, place the lids on top and serve with a salad or a hot canned vegetable.

Gingernut Cream

Preparation time:
15 minutes, plus 2 hours refrigeration
SERVES 8

16 fl. oz. double [2 cups heavy] **cream**
30 ginger biscuits [ginger snaps]
10 tablespoons brandy
4 pieces stem ginger

Whip the cream until stiff.
Dip the ginger biscuits [ginger snaps] in the brandy and place 6 of them in a row in a narrow serving dish.
Cover with whipped cream.
Dip another 6 in the brandy and place them on top of the others.
Cover with cream and continue with alternate layers until all the biscuits [cookies] are used up.
Finish with a layer of cream, which also covers the sides of the biscuit [cookie] and cream layers.
Refrigerate for about 2 hours. Before serving, chop ½ the stem ginger, and slice the rest. Sprinkle the chopped ginger on top of the dessert, and arrange the slices around it.

BRUNCH PARTY

Brunch parties are usually held on Sundays. They have become extremely popular, and guests are relieved of the chore of having to prepare two meals on a day which should essentially be devoted to relaxation.
The key to giving a good brunch party is to maintain the lazy feeling of Sunday, and provide a selection of food which is a happy combination of the two meals. Normal starting time is 12.30 pm. for drinks, with brunch being served around 1.30-2.00.

What makes brunch?
Since the key is informality, guests may congregate in the kitchen to collect their food piping hot; dishes like scrambled eggs, devilled kidneys, kedgeree, sausages and bacon, cold ham with *croissants*, flap jacks, waffles or Scotch pancakes are ideal. Champagne always tastes good at midday either on its own or mixed with stout or fresh orange juice—or offer guests ice cold *vin rosé*, lager, or Bloody Marys, plus coffee, tea and fruit juices.

Lunch parties
Small informal lunch parties are probably the most popular way of entertaining among women, with numbers ranging from four to twelve. The menu should be light and delicious, and two courses are usually adequate at midday. It is pleasant to set the table in a quiet shady corner of the garden in summer, or near an open fire in winter. Start lunch with a glass of sherry or a cocktail and follow with a well chilled Hock or Moselle if the main course is fish.
At weekends when men and children are likely to be present the menu is usually more robust. Definitely a time for old favourites like roast beef and apple pie.

Tongue and Chicory in Cheese Sauce

 ① ① 

Preparation and cooking time:
40 minutes
SERVES 8

8 slices cooked tongue
8 heads chicory [endive]
4 oz. strong cheese
3 oz. [6 tablespoons] **butter**
2 oz. [$\frac{1}{2}$ cup] **flour**
1 pint [$2\frac{1}{2}$ cups] **milk or stock**
salt and pepper

Wrap the chicory [endive] in the slices of tongue and place them in an ovenproof dish. Grate the cheese.
In a small saucepan, melt the butter over moderate heat. Remove the pan from the stove and, with a wooden spoon, stir in the flour to make a smooth paste. Gradually add the milk or stock, stirring constantly. Return the pan to the heat and cook for 2-3 minutes or until the sauce is thick and smooth.
Stir in half of the cheese. Season with salt and pepper and pour the sauce over the tongue-rolls.
Cover with the rest of the cheese and place in the oven for 25-30 minutes.
Take out and place under a hot grill [broiler] for a few minutes, if the cheese is not already brown.

Super Kedgeree

 ① ① 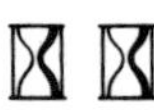

Cooking and preparation time:
1 hour
SERVES 8

8 oz. [$1\frac{1}{4}$ cups] **long grain rice**
1 lb. smoked haddock fillets
4 eggs
2 large onions
6 oz. [$\frac{3}{4}$ cup] **butter**
1 tablespoon capers
4 tablespoons chopped parsley
4 oz. [$\frac{1}{2}$ cup] **cooked, peeled prawns or shrimps**
salt and pepper

Rinse the rice and cook it in boiling water for 10-12 minutes. Rinse in plenty of cold water to separate the grains.
Cook the fish gently in water for about 10-12 minutes. Strain, remove the skin and any bones. Flake the meat with a fork.
Hard-boil the eggs, remove their shells and chop roughly.
Chop the onions and fry until soft in 1 ounce [2 tablespoons] of the butter. Melt the rest of the butter and add the cooked fish and rice. Add the chopped eggs, the onions, the capers, 3 tablespoons of the parsley and the prawns. Mix carefully and season with salt and freshly ground pepper. Place in a hot dish and serve sprinkled with the rest of the parsley.
Kedgeree will not spoil if kept warm in a low oven—250°F (Gas Mark $\frac{1}{2}$ 130°C)—for about $\frac{1}{2}$ hour. Cover the dish with buttered foil.

Cornbread

 ① 

Preparation and cooking time:
45 minutes
MAKES 1 x 8-inch shallow loaf

5 oz. [1 cup] **cornmeal**
4 oz. [1 cup] **flour**
1 tablespoon sugar
1 teaspoon salt
4 teaspoons baking powder
12 fl. oz. [$1\frac{1}{2}$ cups] **milk**
2 eggs
2 tablespoons butter
2 tablespoons oil

Heat oven to 375°F (Gas Mark 5, 190°C).
Sift the cornmeal, flour, sugar, salt and baking powder into a bowl.
Pour the milk into a separate bowl, add the eggs, and whisk well together until thoroughly blended. Add this liquid gradually to the dry ingredients, stir, then beat well.
Melt the butter over gentle heat, and add this with the oil to the mixture. Beat again thoroughly.
Pour the mixture into a well-greased shallow 8-inch dish, or into a loaf tin, and bake for 20-25 minutes or until the cornbread has risen and is golden brown. Serve hot, cut into squares or slices, with plenty of butter and jam or honey.

Variation:
Cornbread Muffins. Spoon the mixture into 12 well-greased muffin tins, and bake for 15-20 minutes.

above: Super Kedgeree
right: Cornbread

TEA PARTY

opposite: far left: Vanilla Cookies
left: Raisin Muffins
below: Orange Cake

The Victorians were undoubtedly the world's greatest tea party givers; it is a pity that nowadays so few people bother to do more than drop a tea bag in a cup and munch biscuits [cookies]. Afternoon bridge parties, committee or fund raising meetings are ideal for those with the time and talent to produce a delicious array of cakes, pastries and imaginative sandwiches.
As with any party a degree of planning is needed. Sandwiches are best made on the same day, but can be prepared twenty-four hours in advance if wrapped in foil and stored in the refrigerator. There are two ways of thinking about bread—elegantly and crustily. Elegant bread should be cut thin, crusts removed and spread with soft butter. Try to keep sandwiches small—if there is a danger of the contents spilling out, wrap the filling roly poly fashion. Smoked salmon, asparagus and egg all make excellent fillings, but whatever you use ensure there is plenty of it—nothing is worse than skimped sandwiches. Crusty bread is best home-baked, very fresh, and not sandwiched. It is more difficult to eat neatly, but tastes delicious.
For cold winter's days hot muffins, crumpets or toasted teacakes are excellent served with home-made jam, or buttered toast lightly spread with anchovy paste or pâté.
Home-made cakes and pastries are difficult to resist. A large cake makes an attractive centrepiece, surrounded by tiny tarts filled with lemon curd or strawberry jam, brandysnaps, meringues and éclairs. A recipe for a simple to make gateau appears on page 62, and Lemon Eclairs on page 61.
For those who like it, it is a good idea to serve China as well as Indian tea, with lemon slices as an alternative to milk or cream. In hot weather iced coffee in a tall glass with a scoop of ice cream makes a refreshing change, or iced tea with freshly chopped mint or slices of lemon.

Raisin Muffins

① 

Preparation and cooking time:
45 minutes
MAKES 15

8 oz. [2 cups] **flour**
3 teaspoons baking powder
½ teaspoon salt
3 oz. [½ cup] **raisins**
2 oz. [4 tablespoons] **butter**
3 tablespoons sugar
1 egg
8 fl. oz. [1 cup] **milk**

Heat oven to 400°F (Gas Mark 6, 200°C).
Grease 15 x 2½-inch diameter muffin tins.
Sift together the flour, baking powder and the salt. Soak the raisins in water for 5 minutes. Drain well.
Cream the butter and sugar until light. Add the egg and milk, and stir until smooth.
Mix the raisins with the flour and add to the mixture, stirring lightly.
Spoon into the greased muffin tins, filling the tins only two-thirds full.
Bake in the centre of the oven for 20-30 minutes or until a toothpick inserted in the centre of a muffin comes out dry.
Take out and cool on a wire rack.

Orange Cake

  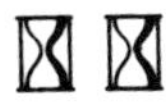

Preparation and cooking time:
1 hour 15 minutes
MAKES 1 x 1½ lb. cake

½ oz. [1 tablespoon] **butter**
2 tablespoons breadcrumbs
6 oz. [¾ cup] **sugar**
3 eggs, lightly beaten
2 large oranges
8 oz. [2 cups] **flour**
2 teaspoons baking powder
For the icing:
4 tablespoons icing [confectioners'] **sugar**
3-4 tablespoons orange juice
For decoration:
10 almonds, blanched and shredded

Heat the oven to 375°F (Gas Mark 5, 190°C).
Grease and breadcrumb a 7-inch round cake tin or a fluted timbale mould.
In a large bowl cream together the butter and the sugar until light and fluffy, then add the beaten eggs gradually. Grate the zest of the oranges and add this to the mixture.
Sift the flour and the baking powder, a little at a time, into the bowl, folding in gently.
Pour the mixture into the prepared cake tin and bake in the centre of the oven for 40-50 minutes.
Take out and leave in the cake tin for 5 minutes before turning out to cool on a wire rack.
Mix 3-4 tablespoonfuls of the orange juice with the icing [confectioners'] sugar, and pour this over the lukewarm cake.
Sprinkle with the shredded almonds and serve when the icing has set.

Vanilla Cookies

① 

Preparation and cooking time:
1 hour
MAKES about 80

12 oz. [3 cups] **flour**
4 oz. [½ cups] **vanilla sugar**
8 oz. [1 cup] **butter**
2 egg yolks

Heat oven to 400°F (Gas Mark 6, 200°C).
In a bowl mix together the flour and sugar. Add the butter, chopped into very small pieces, and the egg yolks.
Work the dough until smooth.
Pipe the dough into strips and cut these into 4-inch long pieces. Shape the pieces into rings and place on a well greased baking sheet.
Bake in the oven for 6-8 minutes until the rings are golden brown.
Take out and cool on a wire rack.

Cinnamon Toast

Allow 1-2 slices of fresh white bread for each person. Toast the bread on both sides, and while it is still hot butter each slice generously. Sprinkle the melting butter thickly with sugar and cinnamon, and serve at once.
Stale bread may be used for another version—soak the bread slices in beaten egg, and then fry on both sides until golden brown and crisp. Sprinkle with sugar and cinnamon as before.

CHILDREN'S PARTY

Giving a successful children's party requires careful planning, imagination —and constant control over the guests. The gold rule is to keep it small and don't make it too long. About three hours is plenty for most 4-11 year olds, with an hour for tea. Organise games like Blind Man's Buff, Musical Chairs, and after tea introduce a calmer note—if you can hire a film projector and children's films, this would be ideal. A quiz or treasure hunt for the upper-half of the age group will hold their attention for quite a time.

bottom: Gingerbread Shapes

Choosing the food
Keep to traditional favourites like small sandwiches and rolls filled with egg, paste, cress, vegetable extract or honey. Provide plenty of cheese straws, crisps [chips] and baby sausages, and remember that children's hands get sticky so avoid large creamy cakes. Offer a selection to drink—orange or lemon, pop, or milk shakes.

Decorating the table
Use paper tablecloths with plates, cups, napkins and crackers to match. Balloons in large bunches make an ideal decoration for the room and can be handed out at the end of the party.

Time to go
Make sure each child gets a small present. It will help avoid confusion if you wrap these in contrasting colours for boys and girls.

Toffee Apples

Preparation and cooking time:
30 minutes
MAKES 12

12 small dessert apples
10 fl. oz. [$1\frac{1}{4}$ cups] **water**
1 lb. [2 cups] **sugar**
12 wooden skewers

Wash and thoroughly dry the apples. Impale them on the wooden skewers.
Oil a baking tray or a large plate.
Heat the water and sugar slowly in a small heavy saucepan until the sugar has melted and the mixture has turned golden brown. Remove the saucepan from the heat.
Holding the skewer, dip each apple into the browned sugar, turning it to coat evenly. Place the apples on the oiled tray or plate to cool. Do not let them touch each other. You must work fast so that you have coated all the apples before the caramel cools.

Gingerbread Shapes

Preparation and cooking time:
40 minutes
MAKES 12

12 oz. [3 cups] **flour**
1 teaspoon bicarbonate of soda [baking soda]
2 teaspoons ground ginger
1 teaspoon ground cinnamon
4 oz. [$\frac{1}{2}$ cup] **butter**
6 oz. [$\frac{3}{4}$ cup] **soft brown sugar**
4 tablespoons golden [light corn] **syrup**
1 egg, beaten
To decorate:
Royal icing (see page 62)
chipped almonds

Sift the flour, bicarbonate of soda [baking soda], ground ginger and the ground cinnamon into a bowl.
Rub the butter into the mixture until it looks like breadcrumbs. Add the sugar and mix again.
Warm the syrup slightly and add, with the beaten egg, to the flour mixture to make a pliable dough. Knead until quite smooth and roll out as thinly as possible on a floured board.
With a gingerbread man cutter cut out the figures. Carefully lift these on to a greased baking sheet.
Give each figure two eyes with the chipped almonds.
Place in the oven and bake for 10-15 minutes, until evenly coloured.
Take out and cool on a wire rack.
Outline the hair, mouth, neckline, and so on with royal icing. Also outline the boys' trousers and the girls' little skirts.

Orange Baskets

  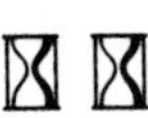

Preparation time:
1 hour
MAKES 8

10 oz. vanilla ice-cream
8 large oranges
1 pint [$2\frac{1}{2}$ cups] **water**
8 oz. [1 cup] **sugar**
$1\frac{1}{2}$ oz. gelatine
8 tablespoons orange squash [orange juice concentrate]
10 fl. oz. double [$1\frac{1}{4}$ cups heavy] **cream**

First cut the oranges into basket shapes. With a sharp knife remove nearly one quarter segment from each orange. Then remove the other quarter segment from the same half, leaving a strip of peel wide enough for the handle.
Scoop out the flesh of the oranges and press it through a strainer, or put it in a blender.
Gently press down the orange baskets to flatten their bases. Place in the refrigerator.
Put the water, sugar and gelatine in a saucepan. Leave to soak for 5 minutes, then stir over gentle heat until the sugar and the gelatine are dissolved.
Take off the stove and add the strained orange juice and the concentrate. Refrigerate until set.
With a fork break the set jelly. Cut the icecream into smallish cubes, combine with the jelly and spoon into orange baskets.
Decorate with rosettes of whipped cream. Serve immediately.

Chocolate-Iced Pineapple Cake

Preparation and cooking time:
1 hour 15 minutes
MAKES 1 x 1 lb. cake

4 oz. [$\frac{1}{2}$ cup] **butter**
4 oz. [$\frac{1}{2}$ cup] **sugar**
2 eggs
4 slices fresh or canned pineapple
4 oz. [1 cup] **walnuts**
4 oz. [1 cup] **self-raising flour**

Heat oven to 350°F (Gas Mark 4, 180°C).
Line an $8\frac{1}{2}$-inch square tin with buttered greaseproof paper. making the paper collar a little deeper than the tin, or grease and breadcrumb a brioche mould.
In a bowl, cream together the butter and the sugar until the mixture is light and fluffy.
Add the eggs, one at a time, mixing well after each one is added.
Finely chop 3 of the pineapple slices, reserving one for decoration.
Chop the walnuts and mix with the chopped pineapple and one tablespoon of the flour.
Sift the rest of the flour into the bowl combining the egg, butter and sugar, and mix well.
Add the pineapple and walnuts and stir until thoroughly combined.
Turn the mixture into the prepared tin and bake in the centre of the oven for about 30 minutes.
Leave in the cake tin for a few minutes before turning it out on to a wire rack.

When cool coat with Chocolate Marquise, and when this has set place the reserved pineapple slice on top. Push the birthday candles into the pineapple and, if you like, stick small coloured pictures around the sides of the cake with a little icing. (This looks particularly effective if you have used a square tin for the cake).

Chocolate marquise

Preparation and cooking time:
10-15 minutes

6 oz. plain [semi-sweet] **chocolate**
3 tablespoons coffee
½ oz. [1 tablespoon] **butter**

Break the chocolate into small pieces. *Put* the chocolate and the coffee into a small bowl. Place the bowl in a saucepan containing about 1-inch of water and melt the chocolate over gentle heat. When completely melted add the butter, stir, and pour the chocolate mixture over the cake.

Savoury Puffs

Preparation and cooking time:
50 minutes
MAKES 24 puffs

1 lb. puff pastry (see page 61)
6 oz. savoury spread
1 egg, beaten

Heat oven to 425°F (Gas Mark 7, 220°C).
Roll the pastry out thinly to form an oblong 12-inches by 18-inches, and divide this into 3-inch squares. Brush the edges of each square with water.
Put a teaspoonful of the savoury spread on to each square, and fold over to form triangles. Press the edges firmly together with the prongs of a fork.
Brush the tops with the beaten egg, and place on a lightly-greased baking tray.
Bake for about 20 minutes until golden, and serve warm.

above right: Toffee Apples
right: Chocolate-Iced Pineapple Cake

BASIC RECIPES

Puff pastry

Preparation time:
1½ hours
MAKES 1 lb.

1 lb. [4 cups] **flour**
1 teaspoon salt
8 oz. [1 cup] **margarine or lard**
8 fl. oz. [1 cup] **iced water**
8 oz. [1 cup] **butter**

Sift the flour and the salt into a bowl.
Rub in half the lard until it resembles fine bread crumbs. Mix to dough consistency with the iced water.
Place in the refrigerator for 15 minutes.
With a rolling pin roll out the pastry to an oblong shape about 9-inches by 18-inches.
Place half the butter in dots on one side of the pastry, folding the other side over. Press the edges firmly together, to seal. Place the pastry in the refrigerator again for 15 minutes.
Turn at right angles and roll the pastry out to a rectangle a little larger than before. Dot again, but with the rest of the lard, fold the pastry over, press the edges together again and place in the refrigerator for another 15 minutes.
Repeat this a third time with the last of the butter, rolling the pastry out to a rectangle about 9-inches by 27-inches. Fold and cool for a final 15 minutes.
Use the pastry as required.

For 12 ounces of pastry
Use 12 ounces [3 cups] of flour, a pinch of salt, 6 ounces [⅔ cup] of butter, 6 ounces [⅔ cup] of margarine or lard, and 6 fluid ounces [⅔ cup] of iced water.

Rich shortcrust pastry

Preparation time:
15 minutes
MAKES 8 oz. pastry

8 oz. [2 cups] **flour**
¼ teaspoon salt
5 oz. [⅝ cup] **butter**
1 tablespoon vanilla sugar
1 egg yolk
2-3 tablespoons iced water

Sift the flour and the salt into a mixing bowl.
Rub in the butter with the fingertips until the mixture resembles fine breadcrumbs. Add the sugar.
Mix the egg yolk with 1 tablespoon of the iced water and add to the flour mixture. Mix well and add just enough iced water to make a firm dough. If too much water is added the pastry will become tough.
Use for fruit pies or tarts, or, omitting the vanilla sugar, for savoury flans.

For 12 ounces of pastry
Use 12 ounces [3 cups] of flour, ¼ teaspoon of salt, 6 ounces [⅔ cup] butter, 1½ tablespoons vanilla sugar, 1 egg yolk, and 4-5 tablespoons iced water. Omit the sugar if the pastry is used for a savoury dish.

Eclairs

Preparation and cooking time:
45 minutes
MAKES about 16

8 fl. oz. [1 cup] **milk and water mixed**
3 oz. [6 tablespoons] **butter**
4 oz. [1 cup] **flour, sifted**
½ teaspoon salt
2 large eggs, beaten

Heat oven to 400°F (Gas Mark 6, 200°C).
In a saucepan heat the liquid and the butter until the butter has melted. Do not allow to boil.
Remove the pan from the heat and quickly tip the flour and salt into the pan. Beat with a wooden spoon until the mixture forms a ball and leaves the sides of the saucepan.
Add the beaten eggs, a little at a time, beating well. Continue to beat until the mixture is smooth.
Put the choux pastry in to a piping bag fitted with a plain round nozzle ½-inch in diameter. Pipe in to 4-inch lengths on to a well-greased baking sheet.
Bake on an uppershelf of the oven for 20-25 minutes, until they are well risen.
Take out of the oven and slit down one side with a sharp knife to let the steam out. Place in the oven again for 2-3 minutes.
Cool on a wire rack.
Fill, when cold.

Variation:
Lemon éclairs. Fill with lemon cream, and cover with lemon icing.

Lemon cream

Preparation time:
15 minutes
MAKES 1 pint [2½ cups]

16 fl. oz. double [2 cups heavy] **cream**
2 tablespoons sugar
3-4 drops lemon essence
grated zest of 1 lemon
2 egg whites
4 oz. [¾ cup] **chopped almonds (optional)**

Whip the cream until thick, add the sugar, lemon essence and grated zest.
Whisk the egg whites until stiff and fold into the whipped cream. Fold the almonds, if these are used, into the mixture.

BASIC RECIPES

Lemon icing

Preparation time:
5 minutes
MAKES 1 lb.

1 lb. icing [4 cups confectioners'] **sugar**
2 tablespoons water
2 tablespoons lemon juice
2 drops yellow food colouring

Sift the icing sugar into a bowl.
Add the water, the lemon juice and the colouring. Stir until it is a stiff paste.
Place the bowl in a saucepan containing hot water and stir until the icing is of coating consistency.

Variation:
Coffee icing. Use 4 tablespoons of water, and 1-2 tablespoons powdered coffee, omitting the lemon juice and yellow colouring.

Basic sponge gateau

Preparation and cooking time:
50 minutes
MAKES 1 x 9-inch cake

4 eggs
6 oz. castor [¾ cup fine] **sugar**
4 oz. [1 cup] **flour**
1 teaspoon baking powder

Heat oven to 400°F (Gas Mark 6, 200°C).
Whisk the eggs and sugar together until the mixture is creamy and thick, and retains the impression of the whisk for a few seconds when this is lifted above the bowl.
Sift the flour with the baking powder and fold very gently, but thoroughly, into the egg mixture.
Pour the mixture into a greased and lined 9-inch round cake tin, or into a greased and lined Swiss [jelly] roll tin, and bake for about 30 minutes until the cake springs back when pressed lightly with the fingertips.
Allow the cake to cool slightly in the tin, loosen around the edges with a knife, and turn out. Remove the paper from the base.
Cut the round cake into three rounds (or the oblong cake into three equal pieces) and sandwich these together with Coffee Cream, or with whipped cream and fresh fruit. Cover the top with Coffee Icing, or with another icing of your choice.

Coffee cream

Preparation and cooking time:
25 minutes
MAKES enough to fill 1 x 9-inch cake

2¼ oz. [¼ cup] **sugar**
2½ fl. oz. [¼ cup] **strong coffee**
3 egg yolks
6 oz. [¾ cup] **butter, at room temperature**

Boil the sugar and coffee together until the mixture turns to a thick and syrupy liquid.
Beat the egg yolks lightly, and then add them to the hot liquid in a fine stream, whisking vigorously all the time. Remove the mixture from the heat and allow it to cool.
Add the butter, a little at a time, stirring vigorously.

Decorative royal icing

Preparation time:
10 minutes
MAKES 1 lb.

2 egg whites
1 lb. icing [4 cups confectioners'] **sugar**
food colouring, if required

Beat the egg whites with a fork until light and frothy.
Sift the icing [confectioners'] sugar and add it a little at a time to the egg whites, beating well all the time. Continue to beat until it stands in peaks when the back of a spoon is drawn away from the side of the bowl.
Mix in a few drops of colouring, if required.

Mayonnaise

Preparation time:
15 minutes
MAKES 10 fl. oz. [1¼ cups]

2 egg yolks
1 teaspoon salt
½ teaspoon sugar
1 teaspoon English mustard
freshly ground white pepper
10 fl. oz. [1¼ cups] **olive oil**
3 tablespoons lemon juice

Make sure all the ingredients are at room temperature.
Put into a bowl the two egg yolks and mix them thoroughly with the salt, sugar, English mustard and plenty of freshly ground white pepper.
Add the olive oil drop by drop, letting it run down the sides of the bowl and beating well all the time until the mixture begins to thicken. Then add the oil a little faster, but be careful not to curdle the mayonnaise.
When half the oil is used up add 1 tablespoon lemon juice. Add the rest when all the oil has been used up and the mayonnaise is really thick.
Taste, and adjust the seasoning if necessary.

Variation:
Curry mayonnaise. Add ½-1 tablespoon curry powder to the made mayonnaise.

CAKES WITH A DIFFERENCE

Creating a cake for a special occasion can be fun, the results can be delicious and provide an original and spectacular centrepiece for the table. We have illustrated a few colourful suggestions and give a step by step guide to the basics involved in creating your own individual rainbow sensation.

The Basics
Each cake consists of 3 differently flavoured and coloured sponge layers, sandwiched together with a variety of fillings, then cut and sculptured into the shape of your choice and imaginatively decorated with icing, glacé cherries, nuts or whatever edible goodies seem suitable. Package cake mixes—which come in a wide range of colours and flavours—can be used, or you can make your own sponge. Whichever you choose you will need cake (or roasting) tins measuring 10″ x 13″ x 1½″ deep, 3 differently flavoured sponge mixes, 2 differently flavoured fillings, a saw edge knife, a bread board or other firm base on which to present the cake, 2 lb. royal icing, 3 shades of harmless vegetable food colouring, a forcing bag with piping nozzle, and nuts, fruit etc. of your choice for decoration.

Basic sponge mix

Preparation and cooking time:
45 minutes
MAKES 1 layer

3 eggs
3 oz. castor [¾ cup fine] **sugar**
a few drops of vegetable food colouring or flavouring
3 oz. [¾ cup] **flour, sifted**
a pinch of salt

Heat the oven to 350°F (Gas Mark 4, 180°C).
Whisk the eggs in a mixing bowl.
Add the sugar and continue to whisk, placing the bowl over a pan of hot water until the mixture has thickened.
Remove the bowl from the heat, add the colouring or flavouring and continue to whisk for a further 5 minutes or until the mixture is cool. Fold in the sifted flour and salt, then pour into a well greased baking tin measuring 10″ x 13″ x 1½″ deep.
Bake in the centre of the oven for 25-30 minutes.

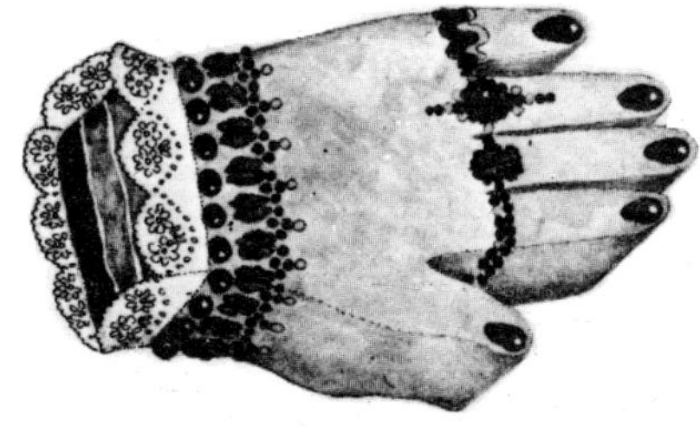

Cream filling

5 fl. oz. double [⅝ cup heavy] **cream**
1 tablespoon castor [fine] **sugar**
a few drops of food colouring or a few finely chopped nuts

Whip the cream until thick, stir in the castor [fine] sugar and mix in the colouring or nuts.

Chocolate filling

1 tablespoon chocolate powder
4 oz. [½ cup] **butter or margarine**
3 oz. icing [¾ cup confectioners'] **sugar, sifted**

Dissolve the chocolate powder in a little warm water. Beat the fat and icing [confectioners'] sugar to a smooth cream, then blend in the chocolate.

Royal icing

4 egg whites
1 teaspoon lemon juice
2 lb. icing [8 cups confectioners'] **sugar, sifted**
4-6 drops of glycerine

Mix the lemon juice and egg whites in a bowl. Then gradually add the sifted icing [confectioners'] sugar and glycerine. Beat until the icing is smooth and firm enough to hold a spoon upright.

How to make the aeroplane cake

Prepare and make 3 sponge layers—1 ginger flavoured, 1 orange and honey flavoured, and the third chocolate flavoured. Leave to cool while preparing chocolate filling and cream filling.
Lay the cool ginger sponge on a bread board, spread it with most of the chocolate filling (reserve a little to use as 'glue'), cover with the orange sponge and spread that with the cream filling (again reserving a little for later use). Place the chocolate sponge on top.
Using a saw edge knife cut out the shapes of the aeroplane (diagram 1). Place the main body of the plane onto the final serving base.
With a sharp knife cut away part of the top of the plane body to form a curved nose-to-tail shape (diagram 2).
Now take the wing piece and slice horizontally through the orange flavoured sponge layer to make two wings (diagram 3). Place the wings either side of the plane body, near the nose end, and secure them to the body with a little of the reserved filling. Place the tail fin in position, again securing it to the plane body with reserved filling. Cut the tail piece horizontally through the orange flavoured sponge to make two tail pieces, place them either side of the tail fin and secure with reserved filling.
Cut the cockpit to shape and secure it to the top of the plane body with reserved filling (diagram 4).
Make the royal icing. Colour most of it with yellow food colouring, divide the remainder between two small mixing bowls and cover each with a damp cloth to prevent hardening. Cover the whole of the aeroplane except the cockpit with the yellow icing, smoothing the icing with a knife dipped into hot water.
Colour one bowl of the reserved icing with blue food colouring, and the other with red. Cover the cockpit with the blue icing, and, when the yellow icing has hardened a little, pipe red icing on body, wings and tail to represent structure lines, and a large initial or name on the wings or body of the aeroplane.
Press silver balls beside the red structure lines to represent rivets (diagram 5). Cut a fan wafer into 3 pieces to make a propeller and secure them to the plane nose with reserved filling. Finish by pressing half a glacé cherry over the join.

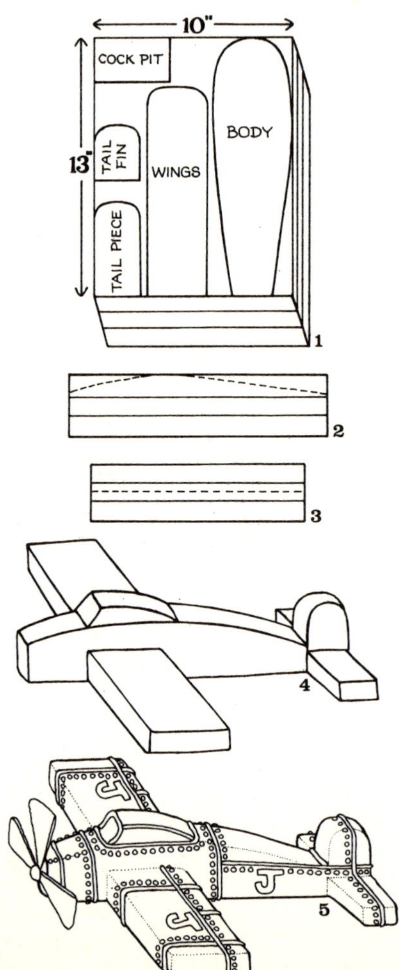